THE DORDOGNE
& LOT

PASSPORT'S REGIONAL GUIDES OF FRANCE
Series Editor: Arthur Eperon

Auvergne & the Massif Central
Rex Grizell

Brittany
Frank Victor Dawes

The Loire Valley
Second Edition
Arthur and Barbara Eperon

Languedoc & Roussillon
Second Edition
Andrew Sanger

Normandy, Picardy & Pas de Calais
Barbara Eperon

Paris
Vivienne Menkes-Ivry

Provence & the Côte d'Azur
Second Edition
Roger Macdonald

Rhône Valley & Savoy
Rex Grizell

South West France
Second Edition
Andrew Sanger

Also available: *Passport's Regional Guides of Italy*

THE DORDOGNE & LOT

Arthur & Barbara Eperon

Third edition

Photographs by Joe Cornish

PASSPORT BOOKS
a division of *NTC Publishing Group*

This edition first published in 1995 by
Passport Books, a division of NTC
Publishing Group, 4255 West Touhy
Avenue, Lincolnwood (Chicago), Illinois
60646-1975 U.S.A.
Originally published by Christopher Helm
(Publishers) Ltd, a subsidiary of A & C Black
(Publishers) Ltd, London, England.

Photographs by Joe Cornish.
Line illustrations by David Saunders.
Maps by Oxford Cartographers.

ISBN 0-8442-9987-1

Library of Congress Catalog, Card Number:
94-69607

Title illustration: the tympanum over the
door in Souillac church tells the legend of
the monk Theophilus' pact with the Devil.

Printed in Italy by Amilcare Pizzi.

Contents

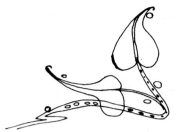

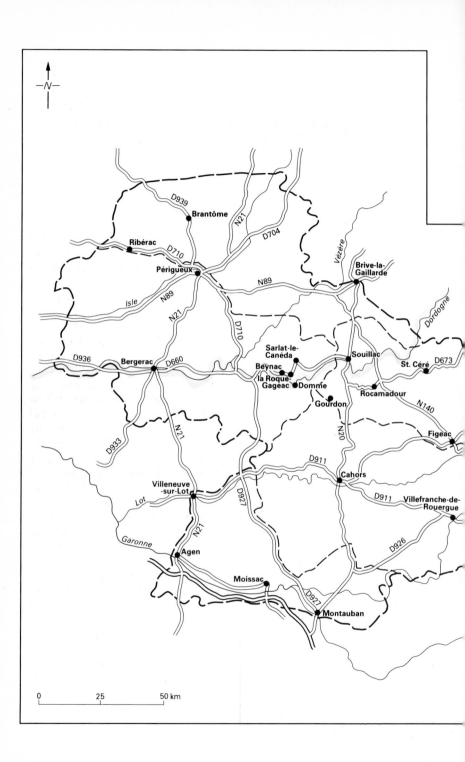

1
Introduction

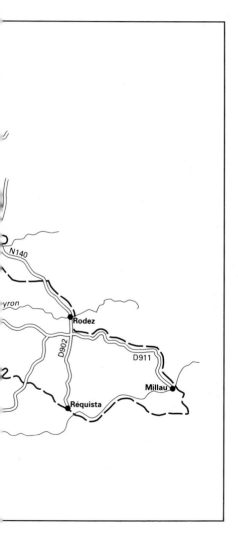

When we first took a good look around the Dordogne in 1952 it was still truly connoisseurs' France, known to some Bordelais, fewer Parisians and a handful of Britons — much like the Dordogne of the 1930s which Henry Miller called 'the nearest thing to Paradise this side of Greece'. Lot to the south-east was almost totally unknown outside France and very little known there. Both départements had even fewer people than when Miller took his holiday there, for young people had gone away to the War or to city factories, old farmers had died, the little farms had become even less economic to work and farms and cottages were becoming derelict. It was a sanctuary of peace, calm, haunting beauty and, alas, decay, paradise to an old romantic or a writer passing through but closer to purgatory to a peasant trying to bring up children in poverty. The young did not so much drift away as run away to enjoy the fruits of the new 'technological France' in booming industrial cities.

Deliberately, as a matter of Government policy, the area was 'repopulated' with tourists, and with Parisians and Bordelais who converted the semi-derelict cottages into second homes.

Now the Dordogne at least is known around most of the world as one of the most desirable places in Europe for a holiday, or for retirement. Except in winter, cars with Paris number plates, cars from Belgium, Holland, Germany and especially Britain, are there in number in every town and in many villages. A few places, like Sarlat, Périgueux, Cahors and Brantôme, can be crowded in midsummer.

Visitors, particularly Britons, speak so loosely of 'the Dordogne' that there is real confusion as to where exactly Dordogne is. They use the word 'Dordogne' to cover anything near the river, even for places like Brive in Corrèze and St. Céré in Lot and for villages way south to the Lot river.

The département of the Dordogne was created in 1790 and is the third largest in France. It covers much the same area as the old province of Périgord, half-way between the plains of Guyenne and the Massif Central. The name of the river was used after an argument about the name for the new département and even today the word 'Dordogne' means only the river to local people. They call themselves 'Périgourdins' and the département 'Périgord'.

People in the Lot département call it 'Quercy'. Napoléon divided Quercy into Haut-Quercy, called 'Lot' and Bas-Quercy called 'Tarn-et-Garonne' and including also parts of Gascony and Languedoc.

Visitors stay on camp sites, in little family-run hotels, but especially in gîtes, those holiday homes which may be anything from a converted barn or a rescued derelict cottage to a modernised farmhouse or one floor of a manor house. Gîte, which means literally a shelter, was the name given by the French agricultural ministry to holiday homes in the countryside, built or converted under heavy state subsidy, to help small farmers stay in business and to bring tourist spending to depressed agricultural areas.

Many holiday cottages or old farmhouses are now British owned and, when they retire, quite a number of owners live in them, selling their homes in Britain.

But Paradise is by no means lost. It is quite easy to lose yourself deliberately or get accidentally lost among the lanes, rolling hills, woodlands, secret hamlets and along the many streams and tiny rivers. You can still spend a day reading and dreaming in a meadow and see nobody but the very occasional passing farmer. The Dordogne countryside is so extensive and still so sparsely populated, the Lot even more so, that a fugitive can always find a hideaway, as many Resistance fighters and escaping Allied airmen did in World War II and many fugitives from telephones, traffic jams and computers do today.

We were staying not long since at the village inn at Larche on the main Périgueux–Brive road and drove 27km to the bank at Souillac, on the busy N20. We decided to take a 'short-cut' back. We drove along little lanes past rich meadows, wooded hillsides, walnut plantations, with only distant farmers at work in fields. We passed through delightful villages with only a few old men and women in the street, and a series of hamlets where the only living creature was a beagle loudly defending the street against our invasion. Then we ran out of road in a farmyard with a sheer drop into a pond. We were only 6km from the busy N89.

There are whole farming areas and

2

Sniffing for Truffles

When November mists come to the Dordogne, you will see farmers setting off on bicycles or mopeds with a dog sitting in the basket on the handlebars or running alongside. In their own secret woods they are going to hunt for the black underground mushroom which grows under special oak trees — the truffle.

This strange magical fungus, which sells for more than most people can afford, can turn an ordinary dish into a gastronomic dream. It is not so much its own delicate taste as the way it brings out the taste of quite simple dishes, like an omelette, poultry, sweetbreads or duck galantine. Curnonsky, called Prince of Gastronomes, said that truffle was a name never used by a gastronome without touching his hat. It was even believed to be the food of love, like caviar. Curnonsky said that it was not a positive love-potion but 'it can make a woman more loving and a man more lovable'.

For centuries pigs were used to sniff out the truffle, but they had a voracious appetite for the fungus and it was often difficult to persuade them to give up their trophy when they found it. Dogs have proved more helpful, if given just an occasional titbit. Anyway, dogs are easier than pigs to carry around, though truffling pigs still exist.

Truffle-hunters can tell which trees the truffles are growing under by the way the grass dies. There are more than 30 varieties of truffle, and connoisseurs will tell you which are best. They vary greatly in size, but the average is about 100g. The biggest recorded weighed a kilo. They are at their best in November when ripe and fragrant. But most of those used in the kitchen come from cans, when they can be used any time. (For recipes, see pp. 148–51).

Truffles appear in November but they are small and officially should not be sold. Early December they are on sale in the markets of Périgueux, Sarlat, Thiviers, Thenon, Terrasson and Montignac in the Dordogne. Lalbenque in Lot has a truffle market in December and January. They are at their peak around Christmas and New Year. The Dordogne cannot supply France's full demand and many truffles are now imported, most from Eastern Europe.

Pigs are still trained to sniff out truffles.

dozens of villages north of this N89 where you can stay in gîtes or tiny village inns. And you will hardly hear a word of English in a week, unless you drive into Périgueux, Brive or Brantôme.

In the Double forest west of Périgueux you will not even find many visitors from the rest of France once you have passed Ribérac. There are many of these areas where farming is almost the only way of life, and if you drive into a hamlet through the little lanes people will assume that you are lost. South of the Dordogne river between Lalinde and Buisson is a secretive hidden world only a short drive from Le Bugue, Les Eyzies and Sarlat. In the hills north of the Lot river above Puy l'Evêque and Cahors, and in the hills and valleys with a maze of little roads south of the river, the people live in a secret world as if the busy, important N20 from Souillac through Cahors to Montauban had never been built.

As you drive around this beautiful and delightful area quick changes of scenery and of agriculture add to the pleasure. Strawberry growing is fairly new but the Dordogne is already the leading producer in France. The mild climate makes it possible to grow crops here and in the Lot which you would expect farther south. There are very few larger farms. Because of the division of land among the family by inheritance, most farms are only 14–20 hectares, and farms are disappearing at an alarming rate. One newspaper said recently that 1,000 farms go out of production every year in the Dordogne alone, and in Lot, around Cahors especially, the stonier, more difficult higher vineyards have long been abandoned.

Truffles, the underground mushrooms which grow under certain oaks (see box), are now outrageously expensive and can make a poor smallholder quite rich for a short time in season.

In old days, a young man taking over a farm would immediately plant a few walnut trees so that his children and grandchildren would not starve. The people lived on bread made with walnut-flour or chestnut flour and dipped in walnut oil. You still see walnut trees in almost every farm, and walnut plantations all over the Dordogne and Lot, with new plantations springing up in the valleys. In France, smoking is not yet regarded as being as anti-social as it is in Britain and particularly in the US. Nevertheless, tobacco-growing is decreasing in Dordogne and Lot, where strawberries have replaced tobacco on many farms. Tobacco-growing is a family business and you can still see tobacco drying in airy sheds.

Cereals and fruit trees grow on the sloping hills of the Brive basin and vegetables and fruit grow in the valleys — a great deal of strawberries these days. In the Garonne and Lot valleys are vast stretches of fruit trees — and tomatoes, asparagus and many different vegetables. Plums are a major crop, and prunes are made by drying plums grown on grafted trees as they have since the Crusades.

Much of the plateau of Quercy is sheep country — 'sheep with spectacles' (black rings around the eyes). Stock raising is becoming more important in the Dordogne département, too — sheep, pigs, cattle for milk and beef. Ducks are becoming as important as geese. You can see whole hillsides alive with ducks in parts of the Dordogne.

Rivers have made the history and the very landscape of the area. The

4

Le Sort, one of the hamlets south of the N89 which still live for farming

Dronne, Isle, Auvézère and Vézère sweep from the hills into the beautiful Dordogne flowing west. The Célé feeds the Lot, which flows west to join the Garonne. And many more minor tributaries wind through villages, hills and meadows to join the larger ones. Above ground, the rivers brought richer soil between the limestone and rocks of the plateaux and for centuries provided the main means of transport for goods and livestock. Below ground, they cut the caves which were home to pre-historic man and which, through discoveries in the last century or so, have taught us more than any other area about our earliest ancestors. From their discoveries, archaeologists have been able to follow the stages of development from our pre-hominid ancestors between ape and man, Neanderthal man living about 150,000 years ago and *Homo sapiens* from around 40,000 years ago.

The Dordogne is one of the longest rivers in France, travelling 500km from its source 1,886m high in the Massif Central at the icy peak of the Puy de Sancy. Five giant hydro-electric dams control the river flow for 120km in the upper reaches between Bort and Argentat, producing nearly one-fifth of France's electricity. Running through Corrèze to Beaulieu, the Cère joins it just below Bretenoux, which is in Lot, and the little Bave joins soon after. Then it turns west and makes those series of beautiful sweeps through rocks and hills called 'Cirque' (amphitheatres) and 'Cingle', which the Michelin Guide calls 'meander'.

Souillac was for centuries the important river trading centre. Timber barrel staves and wine stakes from the Auvergne mountains were brought downriver to the town. They were

5

unloaded and transported downstream to Bergerac, Libourne and Bordeaux, along with wine, corn, cattle and sheep. The boats brought back salt. The Souillac boats were more solid than the other *gabares* (poled, flat-bottom boats) of the Dordogne, which were broken up at the end of their journey for their timber content. Their boatmen would buy a mule and return on it, perhaps selling it to a farmer later.

There were several danger spots on the river, such as Limeuil, where the joining of the Vézère and Dordogne rivers brought choppy, fast-moving waters, and downstream of Mauzac where there is a 100-m stretch of rapids called Saut de Gratusse and many lives were lost. Boatmen needed a pilot until the Lalinde canal was built in the 1840s. After Lalinde the Souillac boats were liable to run into the big Bergerac boats — literally. From Castillon, tides could take them faster to Libourne. The whole Souillac–Libourne journey of 200km usually took three days. Then came the nasty part — taking the boats back laden with salt. Relays of teams of oxen, supplied by local farmers (*bouviers-haleurs*), would normally tow the boat, each team towing the boat for 2–6km. Because of cliffs the towpath moves from one side of the river to the other, so the boats had to cross — with great difficulty. The journey back could take three weeks. Furthermore, the number of days in the year when the boats could travel was about a month, for there was too much water in winter, too little in summer. The larger boats with sails carried passengers as well as cargo. Though many people along the river bank, from sawyers and farmers to innkeepers and boatmen, made a nice addition to their incomes from the boats, the merchants must have been relieved when the Coutras–Périgueux railway opened in 1857 and Brive–Périgueux in 1860. Now nearly all the little riverside villages have beaches, canoes and fishing, and some have camp sites.

The Dordogne river was for long both a thoroughfare and a barrier, albeit a beautiful one. Now it provides power and watersports. The river Lot, too, was important for navigation. The barges, called *sapines* and *gabares*, carried mostly Auvergne cheeses and Cahors wine to Bordeaux. Much of the Cahors wine went to England. Later, coal from De Cazeville was carried. The Lot is truly a meandering river, with a series of snakes and loops which, as at Cahors and Luzech, nearly form a circle, so canals and dams were built to try to straighten it out. Many of the curves are between the tall limestone cliffs of the Quercy plateau. It is a picturesque river, sometimes flowing through fertile fields, sometimes through wild, bare rock.

The Dordogne and Lot countryside is thick with castles, but they are not the pretty hunting lodges and country houses made for sport and love which abound in the Loire. They were built for war and defence and they saw plenty of both. Many were burned down or demolished and rebuilt. Those that survived the Hundred Years' War and the Religious Wars were later either abandoned or converted into country mansions. Many have been restored since the Second World War. But to really understand the Dordogne and Lot, their history and their people, it is just as important and interesting to look at the old farms and old peasant cottages — those that have not been turned into smart weekend and holiday homes. There are still many around.

2
A Little History

The Dordogne and Lot were probably no more populated than other parts of Europe from 150,000 to 40,000 years ago, but we have certainly found more evidence of our prehistoric ancestors in the caves of this part of France than anywhere else in the world. It is not without right that Les Eyzies calls itself 'The Capital of Prehistory'. The rediscovered caves have given up a wealth of evidence of early man's way of living, the tools he fashioned in bone and chipped stone, jewellery and the animals he hunted (mammoth elephants, horses, bison, oxen, rhinoceros, bear, deer and reindeer). Human and animal skeletons have been found, and the most remarkable find of all has been the cave wall engravings, sculptures and paintings, mostly of animals, some of great beauty and realism.

So important is the area that the cultures of mankind during the middle and upper Palaeolithic Period (the 'Chipped Stone' Age) from 150,000 to 40,000 years ago are nearly all given names from the Dordogne and Vézère river area — Tayacian, Mousterian, Périgordian, Magdalenian.

These caves were known to man later in the Dark Ages and in the Middle Ages. They were used as shelters during the various tribal invasions, then

Prehistoric cave-drawings at Lascaux and Cougnac caves.

again when the rival Capet and Plantagenet families were fighting for power
in France and between themselves.
Families took refuge in caves in the
Hundred Years' War, when no villages
were safe from the pillaging troops of
the French, English or, especially, of
the mercenary barons who raised
armies called 'Les Routiers', who
fought and pillaged wherever they
could find the most loot. Many caves
were used, too, as shelters against the
destructive Huguenot captains and
their fanatical followers and the cruel
and ruthless Catholic Leaguers fighting
them.

Then for centuries the caves and
rock shelters were either forgotten or
simply ignored as being dark, dank and
unimportant. Among the more ignor-
ant peasants frightening legends grew
up around them and people were
afraid to enter.

The first significant discoveries of
prehistoric man were found in another
part of France, St. Acheul and Abbe-
ville, by Boucher de Perthes (1788–
1868). But the most significant were at
Les Eyzies-de-Tayac by the Vézère. In
1863 the archaeologist Edouard Lartet
and his British banker friend Henry
Christy discovered in the village of La
Madeleine part of a carved and chis-
selled mammoth's tusk, and suggested
the existence of 'Magdalenian' man.
Lartet made many digs in the Vézère
valley and started to classify the eras of
man's culture. Five years later, workmen digging out the route of the new
Périgueux–Agen railway uncovered, at
a place called Cro-Magnon, the
remains of a family living about 35,000
years ago. So 'Cro-Magnon Man' was
discovered. Gabriel de Mortelit continued the classification, adding among
others Mousterian man from a skeleton

found at Le Moustier near Les Eyzies.

For a common-man's guide to the
various periods of prehistory and the
various tools men fashioned and used,
the Michelin green guide to the
Dordogne is useful. At Les Eyzies, the
Musée National de Préhistoire, in the
castle of the former barons of Beynac,
is interesting and easy to follow. It is
shut on Tuesdays.

Despite the castles, ruined and
renovated, and the bastides with their
defensive walls and their fortress–
churches, it is still difficult to imagine
the terrible turbulence and warfare
which must have made the Dordogne
and Lot hell to live in for centuries —
turbulence that was followed by peace
with poverty.

The Dukes of Aquitaine and Counts
of Anjou of the Middle Ages were
certain sooner or later to fight the Kings
of France, for the Frankish kings, the
Capetians, were set upon taking over
the whole country and the provincial
barons were not only determined to
hold on to their lands and their power
but were often bellicose, too.

With the marriage in 1137 of Prince
Louis, son of the King of France, to
Eleanor, daughter of the Duke of
Aquitaine, it seemed that the French
kings had got more than a mere
foothold in the south-west. For she
brought as her dowry the Duchy of
Guyenne, Périgord, Limousin, Poitou,
Angoumois, Saintonge, Gascony, the
Auvergne and the County of Toulouse.
It was obviously a marriage of conveni-
ence. She was 15, beautiful, intelligent,
loved having fun, patronised the arts,
and liked to surround herself with trou-
badours. As she grew a little older, she
almost certainly became wayward.
Louis, who was soon crowned Louis
VII, was extremely pious and dull. 'I

have married a monk,' she said, despite the two daughters she had borne during their 15 years of marriage.

When they spent 2½ years away on a crusade, they began to live apart. He accused her of having *affaires* and on his return set about getting rid of her. An Ecclesiastical Court met and it was decided that Louis and Eleanor were too closely related to have married under the laws of the Church. It seemed that this mattered more to the Church than her adultery. The Pope annulled their wedding. Eleanor, at 30 and still beautiful, regained her freedom and her lands.

Such a tempting prize was coveted by many powerful lords, including the King's younger brother. One planned to kidnap her. But she slipped back to Aquitaine. She had her eye on a young man she had spotted on some royal occasion who was good looking, lusty and rich. Henry Plantagenet was already Duke of Normandy, Count of Anjou and Lord of Maine and Touraine, and was heir to the English throne. Eleanor sent a message to him. Only eight weeks after Eleanor's annulment, they were married in the cathedral at Poitiers. Henry became Duke of Aquitaine, but Louis VII would not recognise him. His domaines in France were as big as those of the King and moreover, two years later, he became Henry II of England. It was all nearly disastrous for France, and led to fighting which was only contained by the barrier of the river Dordogne.

At first, Eleanor and Henry were undoubtedly a happy partnership. They had five sons (one of whom died) and five daughters. But they were both wayward. Henry had a child by the daughter of Walter de Clifford — the

Fair Rosamund — and he accused Eleanor of sleeping with a troubadour. They fell out completely and Henry shut Eleanor in a tower. That was the saving of France (where a new and more forceful king now reigned — Philippe Auguste), for Eleanor turned her sons against their father. First Henry Courtmantel who had been made joint King of England by his father, turned on him. After Courtmantel's death, the combination of Philippe Auguste and Henry's third son, Richard Coeur de Lion, was too much for Henry II and he was forced to sign a humiliating treaty, whereupon he died in sorrow.

But the alliance between Philippe and Richard, now King of England and Duke of Aquitaine, soon broke down and they fought each other. While Richard Coeur de Lion lived, Philippe made no headway in driving the English out, but when Richard was killed by a stray arrow at a minor siege at Chalus in 1199, his weaker younger brother John was no match for Philippe. The English lands were whittled right away until, in 1259, under the Treaty of Paris with Louis IX of France (St. Louis), Henry III of England lost Poitou. However, he retained the title Duke of Guyenne and held the southern part of Périgord though not Périgueux itself, which was loyally French.

It was Edward I who started the building of bastides in the 13th-century — fortified towns which gave protection to their inhabitants and neighbouring villagers and farmers who could flee there in time of attack. More to the point, they consolidated the English position in their territory. The French quickly started to build their own bastides and it is to both sides that we owe the picturesque and beautiful little fortified towns, like Monpazier and

Bastides

No one is quite sure where the word bastide originated — from bastidas (a Provence word) or bâtir (to build), and no one is sure who thought of them, but these little fortified market towns proved invaluable through the centuries for economic and military reasons. Living in the countryside was a hazardous business in the Middle Ages, and even later with soldiers and robber bands pillaging crops, stealing stock, robbing houses, raping women and killing those who opposed them. To persuade people to stay on the land and work it and to give them a chance to market and sell their produce, lords and landowners had to give them protection. Also, soldiers on the move needed a safe haven for the night.

The first seem to have been built at Lalinde and Villefranche-du-Périgord to the orders of Henry III of England in the 1250s–1260s. The man who built Villefranche for him was Alphonse de Poitiers, not only a Frenchman but the brother of the French King Louis VII, first husband of Henry II's wife Eleanor of Aquitaine. De Poitiers, who was also Count of Toulouse, built a number of bastides. Many more were built under the orders of Edward I of England, including Beaumont and Monpazier, both of which have survived almost unchanged. Domme was built to the orders of Philip III of France — Philip the Bold. But once built the bastides changed hands as their military importance became recognised.

To persuade people to live in the bastides, the peasants were given land outside to cultivate and a house inside, guaranteed protection (which did not always work out), and they were exempt from military service. The little towns were given charters which included the right to hold markets and power over local villages.

The King or powerful lord who built the bastide appointed a bailie as representative. He was judge and tax-collector. The townspeople elected consuls who administered the town's affairs. In the French bastides, consuls were changed annually and wrongdoers were rigorously punished.

The French and English built bastides on the same plan — a square or rectangle with streets and alleys crossing at right angles in grid-iron pattern, with a central square in which there was a market hall (often wooden) and covered arcades around used as shops. The church was often in the main square, unless there was the top of a convenient hill to build it on. Although there were outer defence walls all around the towns, with towers and gateways, the church was usually fortified, too, with strong walls and often four crenellated towers (as at Beaumont) as a final refuge if the enemy got into the town. So a steep hill made it more secure.

Bastides, such as Monpazier, Domme and Beaumont, fought over with ferocity in both the Hundred Years' War and Wars of Religion, are now havens of peace and beauty except in high summer, when not unnaturally they can be crowded with visitors. A good tip is to stay overnight and see them in evening calm and awaking in the morning before the tourists arrive.

Domme, which are some of the greatest delights of the countryside (see Box). Meanwhile, the fanatical Simon de Montfort had been burning and knocking down castles on the excuse that their owners showed sympathy to the Albigensian sect. Originally called Catharists, a faith with its origins in the mysticism of 3rd-century Persia, these Albigensian converts remained Christian but hoped to find perfection here on Earth, not in some future heaven. Albi was their main centre. They lived for a while in harmony with Catholics but they were dangerous to the church and the state, for they did not believe in the authority of the church or the Pope and they were seeking a world in which material things did not matter. They were helped in their campaign of conversion by the corruption and licentiousness of the clergy of that time. St. Bernard set about reforming the clergy and converting the Albigensians back to Catholicism. In 1147 he ran a big campaign in Sarlat, and is claimed to have cured many people of the plague. But he failed to convert the heretics. Their conversion of Catholics spread right through southern France.

In 1208 Pope Innocent III decided literally to wipe out this sect who defied his authority. He chose for the task an Anglo–Norman, Simon de Montfort, a fanatical, ambitious and very brutal man, seemingly with total disregard for human life and property. Viscount of Carcassonne and Béziers, he was also Earl of Leicester, having married the sister and heiress of Robert, Earl of Leicester, who then died. He wanted to be Count of Toulouse.

De Montfort committed appalling atrocities on all the sect, killing off men, women and children. He also seized, and kept or destroyed, castles and manor houses on the flimsiest evidence that their owners were sympathetic to the sect. In 1214 alone he seized Domme, Beynac and Castlenaud châteaux and burned to the ground the castle now called Montfort. He besieged but failed to take Toulouse, his real target. So in 1218 he tried again. During his attack on Toulouse a local stonemason spotted him and threw a boulder at him. It smashed in his head. But the brutal campaign against the Albigensians continued until they were virtually wiped out. To the end, the Pope's forces included children in their mass murders.

The uneasy division of Périgord and the whole of Aquitaine between the French and English could never have lasted. In fact, it would be unrealistic to believe that the English could hold this part of France for very long, despite their great victories. Apart from the distances troops had to be moved even after crossing the Channel, there would always be fewer English, for England had a much smaller population than France then. Peace with skirmishes did hold until the line of Capetian Kings of France died out in 1328 and a Valois, Philip VI, came to the throne. The King of England, Edward III, was a Valois, too — and much more French than English although he is buried in Canterbury cathedral. His father Edward II had married a daughter of the King of France, Philip the Fair, and he laid claim to the French throne. In 1337, Philip VI of France declared the English lands in Guyenne to be confiscated. The Hundred Years' War began.

Edward took his armies to France in 1338. His son the Black Prince won the great victory at Crécy in 1346 and took Calais. The war moved into the Dordogne and the English took Tulle and Domme. Then the Black Death swept Europe, and neither side had time or stomach for the fight as their citizens died in tens of thousands. But in 1355 the people of Bordeaux, determined not to lose their wine trade with England, which was their life-blood, appealed to Edward to help them. It was a superb excuse for the brilliant soldier, the Black Prince, to land in Bordeaux. Next year at Poitiers he defeated the French and took the French King John II prisoner. This persuaded most Périgourdins that backing England was their best bet, and some Sarlat merchants even tried to deliver their town to the English, though their plot was discovered and they were killed. But Sarlat and the rest of Périgord were given to the English under the Treaty of Brétigny, in return for the release of the King of France and Edward III of England's renouncing his claim to the French throne.

There was little but skirmishes for about ten years, then the Breton Bertrand Du Guesclin, who had upset his fellow Bretons by becoming France's greatest military leader, re-opened the attack on the English with fresh troops. The Black Prince's army had been almost destroyed by disease and dysentery fighting in Spain. John of Gaunt, Duke of Lancaster, left London in 1373 with an army of 30,000 men to join the Duke of Brittany, John de Montfort, to fight in the Dordogne; but by the time he reached there disease and starvation had reduced his force to less than 7,000 men. Feeding an army on the move through hostile country in those days was not really practical unless agreements were made with local lords. And then the food had to be bought at inflated prices. Discovering the weakness of the English army when

it arrived and the strength of Du Guesclin's large and well-fed force based on Montignac, the Duke of Brittany went home. Aquitaine was soon under French rule again.

Life for peasants in this whole area of France must have been almost intolerable. Even if they could get into their fields to grow their crops, it was almost certain that the troops of one side or the other or the marauding bands of soldiers, Les Routiers, who sold their services to either side, would steal them even before they had finished the harvest. Houses and whole villages were deserted and ruined. Only the big towns and walled bastides gave any sort of safe haven, and they changed hands frequently. No army was going to feed prisoners unless they were important enough to rate a handsome ransom. They were killed.

The War was by no means finished. Next century Henry V of England revived the English claim not only to Périgord but to the throne of France. His remarkable victory at Agincourt in 1415 was gained with a small army, exhausted and racked with sickness, against a French force three times its size. It was virtually the last great victory of the English archers, who were soon to be replaced by men with firearms. As a result of the victory, and Henry's marriage to Catherine de Valois, the French king's daughter, Henry was recognised under the Treaty of Troyes in 1420 as heir to the King of France, who was already mad. The Treaty was to bring 'perpetual peace'. Two years later Henry was taken ill and died. So did the mad Charles VI. Henry left an infant son, and the Duke of Bedford was made· 'Regent of France'. But the Dauphin, the true heir to the French throne, who had been in virtual exile in the Loire, announced himself Charles VII of France but was reluctant to be crowned. Then Joan of Arc, the peasant girl who believed that God had told her to raise an army and save France, rallied the French, rallied Charles and, with her friend and partner in arms 'the Bastard of Orléans', Jean Dunois, relieved Orléans, and won at Patay. After Joan's death Dunois continued the fight, driving the English out of Paris, Normandy and, finally, Guyenne. The last battle was in Périgord. John Talbot, Earl of Shrewsbury, victor of 40 battles but now 75, marched from Bordeaux to relieve Castillon. Talbot's horse was brought down. It trapped his leg, and a French archer put an axe through his head.

The English still had Bordeaux, but the Hundred Years' War was over. Périgord was virtually in ruins. Quercy (the Lot) was worse. It had been hit not only by the fighting but by epidemics and pestilence. Three-quarters of its churches were abandoned. In the town of Gramat only six people were left. Villages, even whole areas, were deserted. Strangers had to be brought in from the Auvergne, Rouergue and Languedoc to populate Quercy.

Little more than 100 years after the end of the Hundred Years' War the Wars of Religion started (1562) between the Calvinist Protestants and Catholics. Partly because of the poverty there, both Périgord and Quercy (Dordogne and Lot) were centres of Protestantism, and the great Huguenot captain Geoffroi de Vivans was born in Castelnaud in 1543. Henri de la Tour d'Auvergne, of the great Turenne family, was a Protestant leader, too, and companion of Henry of Navarre. Atrocities were committed by both sides and many beautiful buildings were destroyed. Vivans, who got into Domme despite its 'impregnable' defences, by a courageous cliff-climb and a clever ruse, could not resist destroying the church. Henry of Navarre, the great Protestant general, had a number of castles razed so that the Catholics could not use them. Appallingly cruel things were done to simple people in the name of religion. The extremists of the Catholic League formed by the Duke of Guise were particularly vicious and feared, and in the end were fighting Royal Catholic troops of Henri III. In Quercy, the Bishop of Cahors, Antoine Hébrard de St. Sulpice, member of a famous, powerful family who still own the medieval castle at St. Sulpice in the Célé valley in Lot, did manage to negotiate a truce between the Royal troops and the Leaguers.

But it took Henry of Navarre to finish the Wars. He became Catholic to gain the crown as Henry IV but kept the loyalty of his Protestant followers, and by the Edict of Nantes made Protestantism legal. In Quercy he gave the Calvinists four 'places de sûreté' — secure retreats: Montauban, Digeac, Cajarc and Cardaillac. The Quercynois disliked intensely the central rule of Paris and when Henry IV died the people of Montauban revolted. Louis XIII besieged them without success but in 1629 Richelieu put down this revolt which was more an expression of independence than of religion.

Périgord and Quercy were in a state of terrible poverty. The peasants were driven almost to starvation by enormous rents demanded by landowners and the corrupt tax collecting system which lined the pockets of the collectors rather than the King. The downtrodden peasants (the Croquants)

13

gathered in the forest of the Dordogne and marched against the landowners and tax officials, lynching some, destroying property. The leader of the first uprising in 1594 was caught and broken on the wheel in Monpazier market place. But by 1636 the peasants were in revolt again.

The poverty continued until quite recent times. Landowners took two-thirds of what the peasants produced on their land. Families lived on chestnut or maize flour mixed with a little fat and boiled to make miques (dumplings). Harvest failures brought starvation and death to the villages. Peasants took to the forests to scratch a living as wandering grinders of knives, charcoal burners or became goatherds. Even the skilled craftsmen, like basket-weavers, clog-makers and potters, were virtually destitute.

Meanwhile the Revocation of the Edict of Nantes in 1685, making Protestantism illegal again, and the persecution which followed, denuded towns of most of the skilled craftsmen on whom the communities relied to produce their wealth. These people were Protestants, and they had to flee to the Netherlands or England. Bergerac lost half its population. But Périgueux was a centre of Catholicism and it thrived.

The ordinary people of Périgord and Quercy welcomed the Revolution. They were ready for it by 1789. The landowners and governing classes still tried to extract their outrageous rents and the peasants replied by attacking castles and pillaging large houses. They attacked the big, rich churches and abbeys, too, but the local village churches and their clergy were safe, for they too were poor and oppressed. The Revolutionaries in the Dordogne, anyway, were not against the Christian religion but the power and wealth of the lords of the church. Over the door of the old church at Monpazier is still the assertion of faith inscribed there during the Revolution: 'The people of France recognise the existence of the Supreme Being and the immortality of the soul.' But not in those days the rule of Rome.

But the Revolution did not make the people of Périgord or Quercy any richer. The Quercy regions, Haut–Quercy and Bas–Quercy were united into a département called Lot after the Revolution, but in 1808 Napoléon changed that by taking away much of Bas–Quercy and forming it into a second département called Tarn-et-Garonne with parts of Gascony, Languedoc and Rouergue.

Napoléon recruited many of his soldiers from the Dordogne, including generals. One was Yrieux Daumesnil, who lost a leg at Wagram and who, as Governor of Vincennes, informed Marshal Blücher after Waterloo that he would give him Vincennes if Blücher gave him back his leg. There is a square named after him in Périgueux and a statue of him with wooden leg in Cours Montaigne.

Napoléon's bravest and most effective man of Dordogne was from Sarlat. Son of a bar-owner, François Fournier was a patriotic thug: he added 'Sarloveze' to his name in pride of his native town. Even Napoléon found him too overbearing and, despite his courage, gave him no honours, so he plotted against his chief — for which he was banished to Sarlat. But as Napoléon ran out of troops and officers he recalled Fournier, who showed his uncouthness in Spain by galloping into Salamanca Cathedral on his horse right up to the altar. Next he broke down the barricades of a convent, terrified the nuns and then sang mass in a stentorian voice. He was made a general and during Napoléon's retreat from Moscow charged a whole Cossack regiment with a small force. But he suffered frostbite in his feet, which turned to gangrene. Napoléon made him a Baron of the Empire. When the monarchy returned, he succeeded in keeping his barony. Few others did.

The people of Dordogne and Lot backed the ineffective French monarchs of the 19th century and especially the Emperor Napoléon III. Only rebellious Bergerac drew the line at having the Bonapartes back. Seemingly they had changed over the centuries from Protestants to Democratic Socialists. Troops put down the revolt and some Bergerac citizens were exiled to the French colonies.

But still the people of Dordogne and Lot remained very poor. As in Kent, the forest oaks were used as charcoal to produce iron and steel so that the peasants could work their farms most of the year and their forges in winter. But, also as in Kent, coal replaced charcoal, and the forges closed. Furthermore, Napoléon III abolished customs duties which had protected the French industry from foreign competition. People moved away from the countryside to Paris and the industrial towns of the north. Then in the 1850s came an even more bitter blow. Phylloxera, the dreaded aphid which destroys vines, spread from the Midi to the Bordeaux district and then to Bergerac and the other Dordogne and Lot vineyards. The wine-producing business has still not fully recovered. Within a few years two-thirds of the vineyards were out of production, and slow growth in modern times has done little to help.

During the Second World War, this area was at first in the Vichy unoccupied zone, and with its caves for hiding men and materials and the rugged independence of its people, it became a very important centre of Resistance against the Nazis. The RAF used particularly the areas of Padirac and St. Céré as dropping zones for arms, and an enormous number were dropped just after the D-Day invasion. The local Resistance fighters were swollen by refugees from the areas heavily occupied by the Nazis, especially from Belgium and Alsace Lorraine, Refugee policemen from Alsace organised a famous Resistance group called 'Bir Hakeim' which played havoc with German forces as they retreated from the Allies. And it was the writer André Malraux, who lived in Sarlat, who ran the Resistance FFI (Free French Intelligence) throughout France. He used the code-name 'Colonel Berger'. Later, as de Gaulle's Minister of Culture, he set up the Government organisation which protected and restored old areas of towns, cities and villages. The restoration work done in Sarlat was superb.

Alas, with farms growing smaller because of French inheritance laws dividing up property among children, with the French Government's postwar agricultural policy of discouraging farms too small to be modernised and mechanised, and with jobs easy to get for a few years of the post-war boom in the new factories, so many of the young people left Dordogne and Lot that their populations are lower now than 200 years ago. But that, of course, adds to their charm for visitors.

3
Food

There are two ways to eat in Dordogne and Lot — gastronomically and well. To eat gastronomically is, alas, now very expensive. To eat well is incredibly cheap.

Gone are the days when eating à la Périgourdine meant truffles with everything and foie gras in any of a dozen ways. Except in slivers, truffles are now for the rich. Even if you can stomach the idea of eating the livers of force-fed geese your bank manager may insist that foie gras and pâté de foi gras have priced themselves off the menu except for special occasions, and that truffles are reserved for a few specks in pâté or a few slices in an omelette.

But even if the old cookery books do assume that without these two delicious but expensive ingredients you are not tasting real Périgord or Quercy cooking, there are plenty of splendid dishes to satisfy us, from confit of duck and goose (wing or leg of the birds preserved in their own fat) to flavoursome, unusual salads with chopped walnuts and walnut oil, and the superb Sarlat potato cakes.

During a lengthy stay, based on a superb house made from a barn near Le Buisson, found for us by Meon Villas, we discovered one village after another offering good three or four course menus of local food for around 50

francs or even less, and some had duck confit as a main course choice. In Bergerac, while awaiting a repair to our car, we had a meal in a simple little restaurant where the lady of the house did the cooking and served us, and all our fellow eaters were locals. First course was a table of *crudités* (raw vegetables) and the superb Périgord *charcuterie* (cold meats and pâté) with salad. You helped yourself. You helped yourself, too, from the big tureen of home-made vegetable soup placed on the table. There was a bottle of local Bergerac wine on the table, and when we finished that, another appeared. The main course — a plateful of lamb — was accompanied by several vegetables served in help-yourself dishes. Cheese followed — large hunks from a good choice. Then came a delicious home-made fruit gâteau and coffee. The price, including wine, was 59 francs.

With goose, duck and chicken as the main sources of meat, goose and duck fat are used for cooking in place of butter, lard or oil. Even omelettes are cooked in goose fat. In some areas, walnut oil is used for cooking, but that has become more expensive recently — it was originally used because it was cheap. If you are catering for yourself, you can buy goose fat by weight from the butchers or in pots from other shops. You buy confit in tins or jars in its own fat and a simple, delicious way of cooking it is to melt the fat from around it and fry it gently until it has a golden brown crust. Then use the fat to fry or bake slices of potato. To counter the richness eat it with a Périgourdine salad — a green salad with almost anything you like in it so long as it includes chopped walnuts. You can use green beans, curly endive, lettuce, cooked asparagus, cooked globe artichoke hearts, and dandelion leaves if you like their sharp, mustardy taste. It should be dressed in walnut oil mixed with a little wine.

Cheaper pâtés often appear with specks of truffles, cutaways from other dishes. But anything marked 'with truffle juice' means that the juice from a tinned truffle (often brandy or Madeira wine) has been poured in. Beware, too, of very cheap 'truffled' pâtés — trompettes de la morte, black fungi, may have been substituted and it does nothing for the pâté at all.

There are some excellent fungi in the Dordogne and Lot. Cèpes, the delicious round-capped fleshy fungi with a subtle flavour, are delightful when fresh and simply stewed lightly in goose fat, even better à la Périgourdine (with bacon, herbs and grape juice). But out-of-season canned cèpes add flavour to many dishes. Even the dried version retains a lot of flavour. They are often cooked with finely chopped onion and a clove of garlic in goose fat, then simmered in cream. In Sarlat, cèpes are simply cooked in verjus, the acidic juice of unripe grapes used since medieval days as a substitute for vinegar. A few drops are used to moisten another delicious fungus, oranges de César, which is then grilled for four

minutes and served painted with walnut oil. In markets you can see delicate pinkish meadow mushrooms called rosés des prés which are cooked with sliced potatoes, garlic and parsley in goose fat.

The original pommes de terre Sarladaise from Sarlat were sliced potatoes fried or baked in goose fat with parsley and chopped truffle, forming a sort of gastronomic potato cake. They are still served in more expensive restaurants but in cheap restaurants the truffles are replaced with garlic. The name remains the same. In the same way in Dordogne and Lot, ris de veau aux truffes (sweetbreads braised with truffles and mushrooms in white wine and cream) lose their truffles in cheap restaurants. Tomatoes are substituted, and the name varies.

Sarlat is renowned for cooking, probably because it has always been a great market town (especially for goose, duck and truffles) and a wide variety of food is grown in the area.

Game in this whole area tends these days to be domesticated, with boar kept in pens on farms and pheasant carefully reared, so pâté de sanglier (boar), de marcassin (young boar) and de faisan (pheasant) abound in charcuteries, at markets and in restaurants. In Quercy they make a particularly good boudin blanc (soft sausage of chicken and veal). Try cou d'oie farci (stuffed goose neck) if you get a chance. Served cold and cut like a sausage in slices, or hot with walnut oil, it is one of the legion of peasant dishes eaten once for economy which have been refined and have become gastronomic treats. Originally, it was stuffed with the chitterlings of the bird. Now it is usually stuffed with sausage meat and duck liver or foie gras. The old saying was that 'with a neck of a goose, a loaf of bread and a bottle of wine, you can invite your neighbour to a feast'. *Rillettes*, made with pork in other parts of France, are made in Dordogne with shredded goose left over from making confit. They are pounded with goose fat and eaten on bread, with no butter needed.

Thick soups, almost like stews, are very popular. *Sobronade* is still a favourite family dish and is on the menu in winter in cheaper restaurants. Fresh and salt pork are cut into large dice and simmered indefinitely with haricot beans, and other vegetables such as leeks, celery, carrots. It is served over slices of bread. As with cassoulet, the beans make it thick. In Quercy, cassoulet itself is made with confit of goose or duck, sausages and haricot beans.

Turkeys are delicious in Lot. There are still plenty of genuine free-range chickens. They are usually boiled with *miques* added — local dumplings which were the staple diet of poor peasants in the past, when they were made with chestnut or maize flour. Maize only is used now, or else stale bread, worked with egg and pork fat into a ball. Some people add bakers' yeast, and in farmhouses they used to put them under the bed covers to make them rise.

A very nice dish in Quercy is *bresolles*, which is slices of veal baked in a mould with shallots and white wine, layered with minced ham and herbs. In Périgord, pork is made into *enchaud périgourdin* — a cross between roast and pot roast. Loin of pork is boned, salted and left overnight with slices of garlic prodded into it, then rolled. It is partly roasted, then water is added and it is finished like a pot roast.

Sarlat's Saturday market is renowned and Périgueux has one of the best markets in France, but every little town has a market worth attending. At St. Céré's Saturday market you can buy locally tinned and bottled confit, pâtés, turkey and walnuts in season, greengages, cherries, plums, apricots (fresh or bottled in eau-de-vie, to give you a drink and a dessert), and fish from the several local rivers.

Sweet fritters called *les merveilles* are eaten hot or cold, especially on Shrove Tuesday (Mardi Gras). Sarlat has a tasty rum cake, *cajasse sarladaise*. Tins of whole chestnuts or chestnut purée 'au naturel' (without sugar) are used for making stuffings or desserts.

Dordogne produces an enormous amount of fruit and nuts. Peaches, pears, apricots and cherries are often preserved in spirits. Walnuts and hazelnuts are used for flavouring bread and walnut oil, of course, is one of the great treasures of Dordogne — superb over salads. Lot produces superb walnuts, too, as well as plums, melons (Charentais style) and strawberries. But the Dordogne produces more strawberries than any département of France with Vergt, 20km south of Périgueux, the main centre. Peak months for strawberries are May and June but often there is another September crop — and forced fruit is around in March.

In a land so blessed with other ingredients, cheeses are not a great speciality of either the Dordogne or Lot, and some local cheeses seem to have disappeared in recent times, giving way, no doubt, to 'imported' cheeses from factory and supermarket. But Rocamadour has two outstanding cheeses from goat's and sheep's milk. We have selected a few that are worth recommending:

Nuts

In old barns in the Dordogne you can still see the little hand-machines used for making walnut oil and, until recently, in autumn you could still see the older ladies sitting outside their cottages with a tray of walnuts on their knees and a mallet in their hands, tapping the nuts open and extracting walnuts whole. Cracking nuts for the table is still a cottage industry, and the nuts used are usually 'corne', which are easier to crack keeping the kernel whole — important, because broken kernels fetch less than half the price of whole ones. Grandjeu, a local variety of nut, is usually sold broken for making cakes and bread or used for oil-pressing. Franquette nuts are used for all purposes and are the walnuts planted usually in the walnut plant-ations which have been a feature of farming in recent years. When the nuts are pressed for oil, the remains (*pain de noix*) are used for cattle feed. Many years past, the oil was actually used for lighting, as well as cooking, and the wood for rifle butts. Now the wood, of course, is used for furniture veneers.

Walnut markets are held in several towns in October and November. Brântome has one on Fridays, Ribérac on Wednesdays, and Montignac has a Wednesday walnut and chestnut market. Monpazier has a chestnut market on Thursdays and Sunday mornings in October, November and December, and Villefranche-du-Périgord on Saturdays.

Chestnuts are less important as a food because the area no longer needs chestnut flour, but chestnut wood is used fairly extensively in France for furniture. Old-style furniture makers favour fruit and nut trees, including cherry and pear. Beech and elm are used, too, but surprisingly little oak.

Abbaye d'Echourgnac — mild, fruity cow's cheese made by Trappist monks at this abbey at Montpon-sur-l'Isle, Dordogne.

Bleu de Quercy — commercially produced in Figeac and Gourdon, very similar to bleu d'Auvergne — soft, very savoury, blue, cow's milk.

Cabecou de Livernon — goat cheese very similar to that from Rocamadour, produced in Quercy by farmers. Well worth seeking.

Cabecou de Rocamadour — made from sheep's milk in spring, from goat's milk in summer, when it is harder and nuttier. When aged in marc in crocks, wrapped in leaves, it becomes smelly and very tasty. It is then called picadou.

Cabicou de Cahors — local goat's cheese; nutty; best in autumn or winter.

Cubjac — we have not seen this local cheese from Périgord lately. It was made either from goat's cheese or a mixture of goat and cow's milk.

Picaou de Quercy — made from sheep's milk or goat's; when aged in spirit wrapped in leaves it becomes very strong.

Thiers — goat's cheese from Périgord; becoming rare.

With renewed interest in regional cuisine in France comes a revival of 'country' wines, helped by more modern methods of wine-making and inflated prices for more prestigious wines, especially in restaurants.

Bergerac and Cahors reds in particular are recovering their reputation and, by planting more Sauvignon grapes to make drier white wine, Bergerac growers have got a foot into the British market — and the market for lighter wines to go with lighter food.

There has been much replanting in the Cahors area. Some producers are even making a lighter wine to be sold young to accompany 'modern' light dishes. That may please the winemakers and the négociants, who will no longer have to find so much cellar space nor have their capital tied up for five to ten years while the wines mature. But these light wines are simply not in the same class as the traditional heavy dark crimson 'black' wine of Cahors, with subtle perfume, flavour and real distinction.

The best of the new dry Bergerac white wines are delicious. Hugh Ryman's Château de la Jaubertie Bergerac Sec is captivatingly fruity and refreshing with quite a heady bouquet from the small addition of Muscadelle grapes, while his Sauvignon, extra fruity and perfumed, is softened just enough by using 20 per cent Sémillon (see box on the Rymans, p. 54). At the 13th-century Château de Panisseau at Thénac two good white wines are produced — one Sauvignon, one half Sémillon.

One of the great producers of the area is at Razac-de-Saussignac south of Bergerac. He is Pierre-Jean Sardoux, a renowned oenologist from the Wine Institute of Bordeaux, who makes the Château Court les Mûts Bergerac and Saussignac wines. He produces a white Saussignac with 75 per cent Sémillon grapes, a sparkling blanc de blanc, and a delightful rare Saussignac Moelleux (rich, sweet, strong and good value).

His red wines are the new-style Bergeracs. Traditionally, Bergerac producers boasted of the age of their casks. As time passed, the tannin got so strong that not even ten years' maturing could soften it into fruit and flavour. Nicholas Ryman, whose red Château de la Jaubertie has won several gold medals at the great Mâcon Wine Fair, uses a high percentage of new barrels each year. Pierre-Jean Sardoux goes all the way, like the Grand Cru Bordeaux makers, and uses all new oak barrels in which the wine matures for 18 months and will then keep six to seven years in bottle. The tannin becomes softened and the wine beautifully full. The grapes are grown on old vines and 40 per cent Merlot is used — the grape used in Bordeaux — to make wines rich, full bodied, fruity but velvety-soft and easy to quaff.

The Countess of St. Exupéry, whose family have lived and made red, Pécharmant wine in the massive and beautiful Château de Tiregand for generations, now uses 10 per cent new casks every year. This is a good move, for the red Pécharmant from the gravelly hills just north of Bergerac was for centuries regarded as almost equal to a good Bordeaux, and Tiregand was the flag carrier for all red Bergerac wines. But lately it had become a little too tannic. It is aged in wood for 20 months and matures in five years into a deep-coloured, full-flavoured wine. This is the best age to drink it — superb with red meat, game and cheese.

Monbazillac, south of Bergerac, produces the great amber-gold sweet wine made from the same grapes as Sauternes, and once passed-off as Sauternes, though it is richer. It reaches 15° alcohol, should be kept five to ten years and can be kept much longer.

Usually it is drunk very cold as an apéritif, with pâté or desserts. By serving a 10-year-old wine with strawberries, we have made instant converts of people who 'simply do not like sweet wine'.

Côtes de Duras wines from Lot-et-Garonne département between the vineyards of Entre-Deux-Mers and Bergerac are nice fruity AOC red wines like an ordinary Bordeaux and easy to drink young. The crisp dry Sauvignon wines are still fairly cheap and good value.

Montravel is technically in the Dordogne and its red wines are sold as Bergerac but it is only 10km east of St. Emilion. Its whites, made mostly from Sauvignon, Sémillon and Muscadelle, are dry, demi-sec and sweet, have soft fruit and are easy to drink.

Rosette, a semi-sweet white wine from the slopes to the north of Bergerac, is another AOC wine made from Sémillon, Sauvignon and Muscadelle. It is fragrant, full-bodied and is excellent with poultry or fish in a rich sauce, but you are not likely to find much outside the area.

Vins de Pays de la Dordogne, such as those produced around Sarlat, are red (attractive, fruity), dry white (crisp, slightly acidic) and rosé. Coteaux de Quercy Vins de Pays, mostly from the Lot below Cahors, are red and rosé, made like Beaujolais from the Gamay grape, so they are light, fruity, have a bright colour and are drunk young.

Like Bergerac, Cahors was always popular with the English who called it 'black wine' because of its purple colour when young. The Popes of Avignon were addicted, so were the Russians. They still make 'Caorskoie' in the Crimea where Lot vines were planted. Later Bordeaux bought it to liven up pale, thin Bordeaux wines! But

Vineyards at Château de la Jaubertie produce some of the best white wine of Bergerac

Wine Tastings

Bergerac and Monbazillac

Château la Jaubertie, Colombier (53.58.32.11). Take N21 south–east from Bergerac, 8km is sign on right to Colombier with vineyard name.

Château de Tiregand, Creysse (53.23.21.08). Take D660 from Bergerac towards Lalinde; turn left under railway bridge as board of Creysse village appears.

Domaine du Haut Pécharmant, north-east edge of Bergerac (53.57.24.50).

Château de Monbazillac and Cave Co-operative (53.57.06.38). Take D933 south from Bergerac past St. Laurent. Caves on right, château by minor road D14 left after caves.

Domaine de l'Ancienne Curé, Colombier (53.58.32.28). Just above N21, 10km from Bergerac. Tasting booth on N21. Good Monbazillac; good value red.

Château Court les Mûts, Razac-de-Saussignac (53.27.92.17). See Wines; take D936 west from Bergerac, left on D4 at Gardonne, right on D14, then lane left.

Château du Panisseau, Thénac (53.58.40.03). D936 west from Bergerac for 5km, left on D16 to Cunèges, then sign.

Co-operative de Sigoulés (53.58.40.18). Wine of 300 growers, including some good quality.

Cahors

Château du Cayrou, Puy-l'Evêque (65.36.43.03). From Puy-l'Evêque, just before river bridge take little D28 on left, marked to château, which is shown on yellow Michelin. Jean Jouffreau's superb wines.

Clos de Gamot, Prayssac (65.22.40.26). Another Jean Jouffreau vineyard. Planted 100 years ago (see page 23). Marked on yellow Michelin.

Clos Triguedina (Baldés Fils), Puy-l'Evêque (65.21.30.81). On D911, just west of Puy-l'Evêque.

Château la Haute Serre, Cieurac (65.35.22.55). Georges Vigouroux's vineyards; N20 south from Cahors to airfield, signboard points to Hauteserre on D149 left. Audio-visual on wines (English text) and tastings.

Les Côtes d'Olt, Parnac, Luzech (65.30.71.86). West from Cahors by D8 south of river to Luzech, then turn right. 500 growers with some very good wines (les Bousses, Comte de Montpezat).

the dreaded phylloxera destroyed the vines last century, many hill vineyards were abandoned, and not until the 1950s did it begin to recover. After it was classified an AOC wine in 1971, improvement came fast. Made mostly from Auxerrois (Cot Noir or Malbec) grapes, with some Merlot, the Cahors we always knew, called Vieux or Vieux Réserve, has to mature to cask for three years and will keep many years after that. We drank it for years, congratulating ourselves on our secret bargain. Not long ago, Paris found out. A pity. The price went up. It has become something of a fashion in Paris, and, with the other vogue for light young wines, some growers are making lighter wines, and selling them young, called Cahors Gouleyant (almost untranslatable, meaning something like 'easy to drink, light and pleasant'). Don't fall for it. The best growers are making the glorious, subtly perfumed refined wines again, even if it does tie up their capital. You needn't just drink them with red meat, game and cheese. They go with anything except shellfish or dessert.

Of many good Cahors wines, the best we know are made by Jean Jouffreau and his family near Puy l'Évêque at Clos de Gamot, where vines were planted 100 years ago, and at Château du Cayrou which they bought from Comte de Montpezat in 1971 — the year that Cahors wine received its *Appellation d'Origine Contrôlée* qualification. The family has lived at Clos de Gamot since 1610. They use no weed-killers but they have recently changed to the modern method of vinification in steel vats for 18–21 days before ageing in oak vats and then in bottles. The ageing cellar at Gamot was recently decorated with 30 mural paintings showing the history of Cahors and the Jouffreau family since they were first mentioned in 1290. Each year Jean decides personally how long the wine should mature in the wood. At Cayrou, he is helped by his son-in-law Yves Hermann, a truly enthusiastic and knowledgeable young wine maker. The wine is 'gras' — full-bodied, fleshy, rich in alcohol and superb! After much research the Jouffreaus have found and replanted a vineyard famous in the 17th century, renowned last century until the dreaded phylloxera disease attacked Gamot vines in 1882. It was then called Pech-de-Rayet, renamed now Clos St Jean. And it is being worked exactly as it was last century. Everything is done by hand! It is on a hillside near the village of Sals, reached by way of a lane from Labastide du Vert, 7km E of Prayssac along D911. The Baldés family at Clos Triguedina near Puy-l'Evêque have been in the business for eight generations, since 1903. They produce a perfectly balanced wine which fills the mouth. From some 40-year-old vines, they make a special cuvée le Prince Probus, which has a superb smell. 'Un nez profond', one critic said. And that is what the name implies.

Just south of Cahors at Château la Haute Serre (close to Cieurac and the airfield), Georges Vigouroux, one of the great lively characters of the area, produces some of the most interesting wine of Cahors from a hillside vineyard which was abandoned for 100 years until he cleared it of stones in 1971. The wine is fruity, balanced but earthy when young, matures into a heavier, strong and polished wine after about five years. Georges is also an 'éleveur' (raiser of other people's wines), négociant (wholesaler) and exporter, besides owning a magnificent hotel made from a château, Château de Mercuès (see p. 122).

4
Brantôme to Brive

For travellers from the north — Britons or Belgians, Normans or Parisians — the most pleasant way to enter the land we call the Dordogne is through **Brantôme**. There could hardly be a more alluring gateway. This lovely little town enfolded by two arms of the Dronne river is an inspired ensemble of red roofs, narrow streets rich in medieval and Renaissance buildings, stone

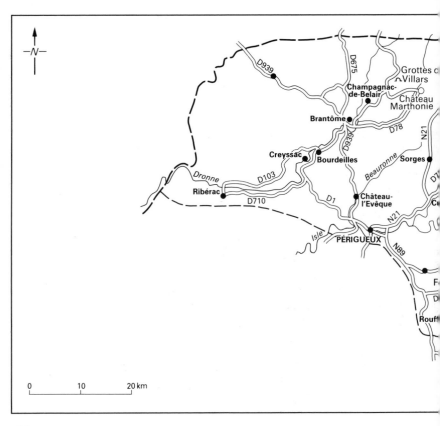

bridges, riverside gardens and shaded walks under weeping willows. It can be a wonderful place to wander, to lean, to contemplate the gently flowing water. Follow the 16th-century dog-legged bridge to the monks' gardens and rose beds, loll outside the old monastery, watch the water tumbling over the narrow weir and you feel already the peace and calm of the Dordogne countryside. 'The Pearl of Périgord, one of the jewels of France, the most ravishing of all the small towns of Périgord,' wrote André Maurois.

Alas, not always these days. For such a jewel has its admirers — millions of them, and in high summer car and coachloads of sightseers cram the narrow streets of the old town, especially on market day. Trying to find a parking space can destroy your peace of mind even before you start to explore.

Go in spring or autumn when there is room to browse and the Tuesday market is for local villagers and farmers come to buy and sell. It is a splendid market for food, selling all the delicacies of the Périgordian countryside, from pâté, duck and goose confit and goose fat to superb *chanterelles*, *cèpes* and *morilles* mushrooms — and truffles, of course, for the rich. Brantôme is particularly blessed with good hotels

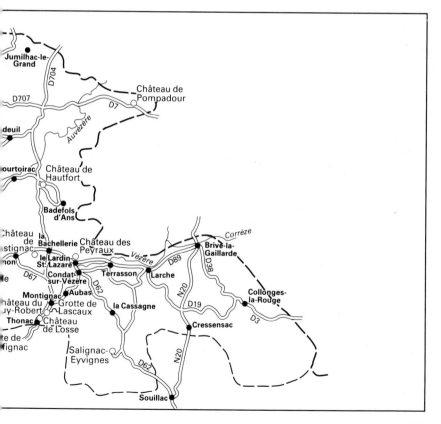

25

and restaurants, with Régis Bulot's romantic riverside mill, Moulin de l'Abbaye and Jean-Claude Charbonnel's Chabrol by the river bridge leading the way, and the little Auberge du Soir, with simple rooms and regional dishes, leading the pack.

The monastic buildings of the abbey are now used as the town hall, museum and school, so they are open to the public only from 1st June to 15th September, which is a pity. But the church is open, and the gardens, and the buildings reflected in the river are a lovely sight. Charlemagne founded a Benedictine abbey here in 769 but the dreaded Norsemen sailed up the river and sacked it. It was rebuilt in the 11th century and altered greatly in the 14th and 18th centuries. It was in the 14th century that two cupolas in the church were replaced by Angevin vaulting. The church is plain but its 11th-century bell-tower, square and gabled and built on a sharp towering rock 12m high, is a delight. Roofed in stone slates, it has four storeys, with round arches. Caves beneath were used by the monks as a bakery and wine cellar. They have huge 16th-century bas-reliefs carved in the rock. One is of the Last Judgement — a hint perhaps to the monks not to overdo the wine.

The museum in the abbey buildings, open Easter to 31st October, contains a few prehistoric finds and little of interest except strange amateurish pictures by a local engraver–artist, Fernand Desmoulin (born 1853), who is said to have painted under the influence of a medium, who was obviously not a great artist. The old monastery has a beautiful 17th-century staircase.

The abbey is remembered for its commendatory abbot, Pierre de Bourdeille, known as Brantôme, wit, satirist, chronicler of scandals and gossip at the French courts in the 16th century. Son of a Count, he was made abbot at the age of 16 by Henry II, but never took Holy Orders. He became a soldier of fortune — a genuine 'freelance' — and courtier, and in 1561 he accompanied the young Mary Stuart back to Scotland after the death of her husband, the Dauphin of France. Then he went to Malta to help the Knights of St. John fight Suleiman the Magnificent. He fought in Italy for the French, in Africa for the Spaniards and in Hungary against the invading Turks. Made Chamberlain to Charles IX and Henry III, he fought against the Protestants at Jarnac but, after a crippling fall from his horse, returned to Brantôme abbey to write his chronicles. By diplomatic persuasion, he twice saved the Abbey from Protestant destruction in the Wars of Religion. He died in Brantôme in 1614. The edition of his chronicles published in the 1890s runs to 13 volumes.

He is buried in the chapel of **Château de Richemont** which he built near St. Crépin-de-Richemont. The château is open only mid-July to August. Far more impressive is the château where he was born — **Château de Bourdeilles**, 10km down the very attractive route by D78 then D106 SW from Brantôme, running alongside the river Dronne. The river here is lined with poplars and walnut trees and passes below cliffs indented with shelters used by prehistoric men.

Bourdeilles is a delightful little place with an impressive and interesting castle. The white houses with red roofs line the shallow but swift river right under the walls of the great high castle which is part medieval fortress and part Renaissance house. Crossing the river

Abbey and church of St. Peter by the river Dronne at beautiful Brantôme.

below it is a curved medieval bridge beside an old fortified watermill built like a ship. The wheels still turn.

In the 13th century the Barony of Périgord and Bourdeilles was ceded to the English by the French King Louis IX (St. Louis), and that caused terrible problems in the Bourdeille family (the name of the town carries an 's' at the end, that of the family does not). The elders of the family supported the English Plantagenets; the younger branch, the Maumonts, supported the French Capetian royal house. After plots and lawsuits, Géraud de Maumont seized the castle and King Philip IV (Philip the Fair) turned Bourdeilles into a formidable fortress inside English-owned territory. Maumont rebuilt the 12th-century fortress and it was called the 'new château'.

The Renaissance house was built in a hurry by Jacquette de Montbron, wife of Comte André de Bourdeille and sister-in-law of Brantôme, the soldier– writer. Jacquette was expecting a visit from Catherine de Médicis who was taking her young son Charles to see something of his kingdom, and she built the new house for them and the court. But Catherine did not arrive and building stopped.

There are superb views of the town, river and old bridge from the castle terrace and watch-path.

Furnishings in the Renaissance buildings were brought here from the château of la Treyne. The chests are interesting: they include some from the 15th and 16th centuries as well as corsairs' sea chests. The Gold Room on the first floor is ostentatiously deco-

Riverside houses at Brantôme

Brantôme — 16th-century elbow bridge over the river Dronne and the historic abbey, now the town hall

rated with a superb ceiling, fine woodwork and paintings by Ambroise Le Noble, one of the 16th-century court artists from Fontainebleau. On the second floor are Spanish paintings and furniture, including the gilded and sculpted bed of Charles V.

Altogether, Bourdeilles is a place not to miss, especially as the attractive riverside road continues past Creyssac to meet the little D1, on which you can cut across the countryside to Périgueux. Or you can continue past D1 on more pretty roads (D103, D104E) to reach **Ribérac**, centre for gîtes holidays and walnuts. It holds a walnut market every Wednesday from October to December, an agricultural market every Friday, a market for wickerwork

and baskets weekly from May to September and several other large fairs at various dates. In a château long since gone, the 'greatest of troubadours', Arnaut Daniel, was born. You may meet several Britons in the markets and shops, for this is a favourite area for the British to buy houses.

The D939 Brantôme to Périgueux road is attractive, too, but has more traffic and misses Bourdeilles. It does go through Château-l'Evêque, where the 14th-century château overlooks the Beauronne valley.

Just 6km north-east of Brantôme at **Champagnac-de-Belair** is a truly idyllic tiny country hotel, Le Moulin du Roc. Lucien and Solange Gardillou created a minor masterpiece from a 17th-century

André Maurois (1885–1967)

In the 1914–1918 War, André Herzog, novelist and biographer who wrote under the name of André Maurois, shared tent, rations and bath tub for six months with a British officer who was polite enough to ask him absolutely nothing about his personal life. Maurois came to admire this British reticence and under-statement so much that he wrote a novel called *The Silences of Colonel Bramble*, which was an immediate best-seller in France and England.

After the war, he married Simone de Caillavet and lived at Château d'Essendiéras. Though living in Périgord and enthusing in conversation and in print on the beauties and joys of the local countryside and its food, he wrote prolifically about the English, trying to make the French understand them, which he personally did.

'If you have crossed the Atlantic alone in a small boat,' he advised Frenchmen, 'say to an Englishman that you do a little sailing.' He wrote lives of Queen Victoria, Edward VII, Disraeli, Shelley (the great book *Ariel*), Byron, the actress Mrs Siddons, the Imperialist Cecil Rhodes and the discoverer of penicillin, Sir Alexander Fleming. And he worked tirelessly to bring England and France together, not for military and political necessity but for the sake of people in both countries.

He might be disappointed now. But he would surely approve of the still-growing love of the British for the Périgord countryside and its food.

nut-oil mill, standing in gardens beside a little stream. The old machinery is still there, outside and in the little lounge. The intimate dining room and beamed salon are exquisitely furnished in antiques, as are the bedrooms. Solange's cooking is superb, too.

Just 6km north-east of Champagnac are sites worth visiting. **Puyguilhem** château looks as if it has strayed from the Loire. It was built in the early 16th century by Mondot de la Marthonie, first president of the Paris *parlement* and a chief minister to Louise de Savoie, when her son Francis I left her as regent while he was in Italy. Mondot's son finished the château but it was in a terrible condition when the State took it over and restored it after World War II. There is a massive round

tower at one end of the main building and at the other a tower built to house the main staircase. It has recently been furnished with pieces from other State châteaux and is open from 1st February to 15th December. It is an elegant château, but rather over-praised by some guides.

Eight kilometres east at St. Jean-de-Côle is another château built by the same family, **Château Marthonie**, which houses a collection of publicity posters and a demonstration of hand-made paper. The village on the Côle, a tributary of the Dronne, is charming, with old houses, a narrow hump-backed bridge, and an unusual 11th-century priory church.

The **Grottes de Villars** (Villars Cave's), 4km north–east of Puyguilhem, were the homes of a prehistoric family or tribe, during the Aurignacian (Upper Palaeolithic) age nearly 40,000 years ago. They left behind engravings and paintings coloured with manganese oxide. The caves have stalagmites, stalactites and other translucent concretions.

Much of the D78 and D707 roads eastward from Brantôme to Thiviers is attractive. **Thiviers** is another little town with lots of markets and fairs. The Saturday market is renowned for poultry, sausages, foie gras and, in season, truffles. Luckily, the busy N21 skirts the town and it is worth walking around to explore the old houses, the much-restored Château Vaucocour which looks down on the valley of the river Isle from towers and turrets, and its lovely church built from the 12th century onwards, with strange Romanesque sculptures. Monsters swallow people, who cling helplessly to branches, other men flee, a bird attacks a man picking grapes; but Samson is overcoming a lion. How they must have frightened medieval congregations!

Excideuil, south-east of Thiviers, is quite a lively and charming town, especially during Thursday markets. The fountain in the market square was a gift of the local boy who made good — Marshal Bugeaud, who conquered Algeria. The château is splendid, but, alas, cannot be visited. The Viscounts of Limoges built it in the 11th to 12th

Pompadour

In 1745, Louis XV gave the 15th-century château of Pompadour to his mistress Antoinette Poisson, beautiful, intelligent, patroness of the arts, founder of Sèvres china manufacturing, and arbiter of fashion. With the château came the title of Marquise and she became Madame de Pompadour. She ceased to be Louis' mistress after four years. It seems that he enjoyed it more than she did and so she found him a series of unimportant girl-friends to lie-in for.her. But she remained his friend and confidant and had enormous influence on France's finances (which hit very low ebb) and on its foreign policy (with the Seven Years' War, so disastrous to France, the loss of French Canada, French India and most of the French West Indies to the British). But her influence has been exaggerated, for the other confidant of the King was Richelieu, and they were hated rivals. She never visited the château. When she died in 1764, aged 40, Louis established a stud at Pompadour. Known as the 'City of the Horse', it became the stud in the 19th century of Anglo-Arab horses introduced from Britain. Now around 100 stallions of many breeds are stabled here. Race meetings and shows are held in summer. The château is used for administration and personnel of the stud and only the terraces are open to the public, but you can visit the stables in the afternoons and on Sunday mornings from 2nd July–28th February.

Incidentally, Pompadour claimed to keep her sexual charms by stuffing herself with truffles and chocolates.

Bourdeilles is one of the most attractive and interesting little towns in France

Riverside garden of Moulin du Roc at Champagnac-de-Belair near Brantôme, old water mill, now a delightful hotel

centuries during their rivalry with the Counts of Périgord. Richard Coeur de Lion failed three times in 1182 to take it, but inevitably the English did finally take it in 1356 during the Hundred Years' War and equally inevitably the Breton, Bertrand du Guesclin, took it back. He was the likeable hero who defeated the English on many occasions but was still so liked by them that when they captured him he lived at Court in London until ransomed. François de Cars, who bought the château from

Henri III in 1582, turned it into a superb Renaissance home.

Château d'Essendiéras, close to nearby St. Médard-d'Excideuil, was the home for a long time of André Maurois, the writer whose works included *The Silences of Colonel Bramble*, the portrait of an Englishman in the First World War (see box on page 30). He came here after the death of his wife Janine to stay with friends and to hide his grief. He fell in love with the Pèrigord countryside and then with the daughter

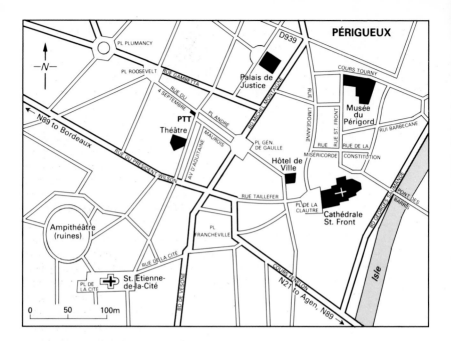

of the château, Simone de Caillavet. They married.

The very attractive D78 runs from the N21 just north of Thiviers through delightful hamlets and country to **Jumil-hac-le-Grand**. In a spectacular setting on a jutting rock overlooking gorges of the river Isle is a 13th-century castle built by the Knights Templars. In 1579 the Chapelle family, local ironmasters and arms makers, bought it and crowned it with a forest of pointed and pepper-pot towers and turrets, which they topped with forged iron birds, cupid, angels, sun and moon. In the 17th century two wings were added and a balustraded balcony, and from the town this architectural hotch-potch looks quite remarkably impressive and even romantic, especially when floodlit in the tourist season. There are guided visits daily from 1st July to 15th Septem-

ber and you can visit it on Sunday afternoons from 15th September–15th November and 15th March–1st July. You will see a tiny closet with remains of simple wall paintings, called the Spinner's Room. Louise de Hautefort was imprisoned in this room for being unfaithful to her husband, Antoine. She passed the time spinning, painting the walls and making love to her boyfriend, who was smuggled in disguised as a shepherd. She wore a big lacy pinafore, rumoured to be big enough to hide her lover in emergencies.

Just over the border in Corrèze eastward is the **Château de Pompadour**, given by Louis XV to his beautiful and intelligent mistress, Antoinette Poisson (see box). It is now a National Stud, which you can visit and where race meetings are held.

The majestic hilltop 17th-century

Château de Hautefort south-east of Excideuil is more like a love palace of the Loire than a fighting château of Périgord. It dominates the countryside, which is beautiful around here. Burned out in 1968, it has been restored by the Baroness de Bastard, whose family home it is. Entering by a drawbridge on which flowers grow, you reach a courtyard with living rooms on three sides and the fourth open to the village which huddles beneath the walls. One tower contains a chapel with the altar from the coronation of Charles X. The other has a museum of the writer Eugène Le Roy (1836–1907), who was born at the château when his father was bailiff. Le Roy was very much a writer of the Dordogne, where most of his novels were set — among the peasants, farm workers and hamlets. After army service abroad, Le Roy became a tax collector based in Domme and Montignac. He had a real understanding of the peasants' problems: the landowners were his villains. His best known novel, *Jacquou le Croquant*, was about a peasants' revolt against their appalling poverty.

The tapestry room has fine tapestries from Flanders and Brussels. One of the joys of a visit is to walk through the beautiful 30-hectare park to the terraces, from where there are lovely views. Part of the château, the gardens and terraces are open daily from Palm Sunday to 1st November, and Sunday afternoons only the rest of the year.

The château has had a violent history. The original 12th-century castle belonged to the Born family. Bertrand de Born, troubadour–knight, wrote songs of love and war. He was mentioned by Dante in the *Divine Comedy*, but not to his advantage. He frequented the court of the intelligent, attractive and wayward Eleanor of Aquitaine, wife of King Louis VII of France, then of Henry Plantagenet, Henry II of England, and she was supposed to be rather friendly to troubadours. He wrote pointed satirical verses which caused havoc among the Plantagenets. When Bertrand and his brother Constantin were fighting over the château, Bertrand had the help of Henry II and of Eleanor's eldest son Henry, the 'Young King'. So Constantin called in another son, Richard Coeur de Lion. Bertrand held it but when the Young King died Constantin returned with Richard and took it. Bertrand conned old Henry II into giving him back the château, but when he was away Constantin returned and destroyed it. Bertrand gave up and became a monk. Perhaps he was repenting for all the damage his verses had done in setting man against man — and woman. The Hautefort family, who had taken over in the 15th century, built a new château in the 17th century.

Minor roads in this area are very attractive, and you have a choice of two nice routes southward to **Badefols d'Ans**, a pretty tiny market town with good views, a 12th-century domed church, and a pleasant real old village inn, les Tilleuls, with bargain meals. The 14th-century château which has great character was burned by the Germans as they retreated in 1944, but stood up to it well and has been restored. That addition of 'd'Ans' to several village names around here came from a Flemish lord of Ans, who married an Hautefort daughter and took these villages as her dowry.

The maze of roads between the D705 and N89 take you through true farming country and little villages where

Byzantine-style cathedral at Périgueux, much altered in 'restoration' last century by the architect of Sacré-Coeur

few tourists penetrate. This is like the old Périgord of 30 years ago. The D5 from just north of Hautefort almost alongside the Auvézère river to Perigueux is a delightful road for slow wandering, with stops perhaps at one or two of the village inns where cheap meals of regional dishes are served, such as the Poste or Des Voyageurs right beside the river at Tourtoirac, or the corner café in the square of the charming little town of Cubjac.

Further north, although it is on the fairly busy N21, **Sorges** is a pleasant market town, almost as well known for truffles as Sarlat. It now has a truffle museum in the Syndicat d'Initiative, with maps, tables, photos and books, and a film on hunting these precious 'Black Diamonds' with dogs and pigs. The museum is open afternoons except Tuesdays; you can buy truffles in the shop. A one hour walk (2km) to the truffle beds under truffle oaks has been mapped out from Sorges.

Périgueux is a perplexing place. The white domes of the cathedral, as you enter this capital of Périgourdine food, promise also an architectural feast. The promise is especially clear if you come in from the south, driving over the river Isle into Cours Fénelon. From the bridge you can see much of the town. Then you tangle with some fearsome traffic and pass a higgledy-piggledy mess of buildings and you think that this is just another uninspired provincial town used simply for business, shopping and money making, where a lot of the old has been destroyed, and replaced by nothing memorable, except some wide boulevards already bursting with traffic.

But get out and walk. Explore the old town around St. Front's cathedral, walk the steep, cobbled, narrow medieval streets where you meet few other visitors and discover buildings with Renaissance turrets, delightful courtyards, Renaissance staircases and balconies, and you realise that the old city is still there, restored with sympathy. And this is no tourist area. People live and work in these old houses. Go to place de la Clautre on Wednesday or Saturday mornings and there right in front of the cathedral is a big market serving the surrounding countryside, traditional but living proof that this is the capital of Périgord. Stay a few days, eat those superb Périgourdin dishes in local restaurants, browse in the shops of the old quarter, and you will catch some of the spirit of this very old city — which has withstood terrible misfortunes in an area of France which was a battleground for centuries.

The large curious cathedral, third church on this site and finished about 1173, seems to have strayed from Constantinople or even St. Mark's Square in Venice. In Byzantine style, it has five domes topped by cupolas, with more cupolas peering from between them. The bare but grand interior with its enormous pillars and high domes is hung with 'Byzantine' chandeliers, designed last century. It is vast and cold, like stone wine cellars stripped of their bottles.

It is really two churches joined by a tall belfry. Of the church consecrated in 1047, there remain four bays. It was burned out in 1120 and the new church, designed to incorporate it, was built in the plan of a Greek cross with five cupolas, said to have been based on the former Church of the Apostles in Constantinople. In 1575, during the Wars of Religion, Protestants entered the town disguised as peasants attending the market and pillaged the cathedral. Over centuries the building became dilapidated and was patched up and 'restored' with little sense of the original.

In 1852, it was decided to start thorough restoration, Viollet-le-Duc, the man who rebuilt Carcassonne, wanted the job. Instead it was given to Paul Abadie, an extremely controversial architect who had a habit of redesigning under the cloak of restoring. Many fellow architects called him 'The Wrecker'. He was either a big-headed barbarian or a bold, enlightened innovator, according to your personal opinion. He certainly interpreted his restoration-brief at Périgueux very widely. He decided to rebuild almost everything. He added 17 turrets. To give the cathedral a more geometric shape, he removed a Romanesque refectory. He replaced Romanesque decoration with a 19th-century version. The original carvings are now in the Périgueux museum. One wonders what would have happened if an architect had decided to add a forest of turrets to a cathedral like York Minster after war damage.

Abadie's work caused much indignation in Périgord, but not, it seems, in Paris, for he was given the job of designing the cathedral of Sacré-Coeur. And he based it on St. Front's in Périgueux!

They are still restoring the church which was the cathedral until 1669 — the church of St. Etienne-de-la-Cité. Originally it was roofed in the 12th century with a line of four domes, but the Protestants took down two and left only two bays. It was restored in the 17th century, then damaged during the Fronde period (1649–1653) when the forces of the aristocrats rebelling

Collonges-la-Rouge

The intriguing tiny medieval town of Collonges was called 'La Rouge' because of its red sandstone buildings. Despite the crowds who come to admire it, the town has kept much of its old charm and looks, even to the badly paved roads, lined by 15th-, 16th- and 17th-century houses — some now restaurants. The 12th-century church is fortified and has a gun-room communicating with the watch-path on the battlements — a very wise precaution in the Hundred Years' War. Heavily fortified, too, is the elegant 16th-century house of the viscounts of Turenne-Vassignac, which is liberally supplied with large towers, turrets, watch towers and defensive loopholes. Many of the old houses have defensive turrets and are fortified.

It is a splendid place for walking around, so leave your car by the old railway station and have a meal at the attractive Relais St. Jacques de Compostelle or the charming flower-decked Auberge le Prieuré.

against Royal power laid siege to the town and had actually placed a pile of faggots ready to light under the tower of St. Front cathedral when the Royalist troops arrived. St. Etienne was secularised during the Revolution but reconsecrated under Napoléon I when he was Emperor. It stands in what is now the modern part of the city. So does the remains of a Roman arena which once held 20,000 spectators. An 11th-century Count of Périgord built a fortress in the arena. Later, the townspeople removed the stones to build houses. Now the remains are in the middle of a big, busy square.

The Renaissance houses which are left are truly worth seeing. The best are in rue Limogeanne, rue de la Constitution, de la Clarté, Barbecane and Miséricorde.

The N89 road from Périgueux to Brive-la-Gaillarde, just over the Corrèze border, is busy in summer and not outstandingly attractive, but you only have to wander a little way from it on the minor roads to the north or south and you find tiny agricultural villages among the pleasant lanes of the hills and valleys. And the superb Grotte de Lascaux is only 10km off the road.

Rouffignac is reached from N89 on little roads through the forest of Barade, which has pleasant marked walks. Rouffignac was systematically burned down by retreating Germans, in 1944, in pique for the successes of the French Resistance. The 1530 church alone survived. The village has been rebuilt and is in a pleasant setting among gentle hills. Five kilometres south is the oldest-known cave in France (known as early as the 15th century) **Grotte de Rouffignac** or Cro de Granville. A dry cave, it is 8km long, but you are not expected to walk it. You can see the best of the galleries on a 4km tour by electric train, and the prehistoric engravings of horses, ibex, bison, rhinoceros and mammoths are worth seeing, but suspiciously numerous. Some archaeologists believe that a number have been added over the centuries. But at least the majority are genuine, from the Magdalenian Age.

Terrasson, centre of truffles and walnuts, rises in terraces from the Vézère river

The first market town along N89 is **Thenon**, where people of the villages shop. Its market is completely genuine, not pandering to tourists in any way, and it is a good place to buy simpler regional food, like country pâté, cheese and vegetables. There is a pleasant little lake where you can take out a rowing boat, swim or get a snack lunch with wine from a hut. The D67 takes you down to **Montignac**, terraced up a hillside above the attractive Vézère river, a place made famous in 1940 by the discovery of wonderful paintings with

which some prehistoric men decorated the nearby caves of **Lascaux**. Alas, since 1963 the caves have had to be closed to the public, for visitors introduced bacteria, algae and carbon dioxide from their breath which would have destroyed the paintings which have lasted about 17,000 years. Now, you must be content with Lascaux II, in a disused quarry about 250m from the original caves. Here, with the help of stereoscopic pictures and computers, a painter Monique Peyrac has produced the two most important galleries of the

The busy town at Brive-la-Gaillarde retains houses from several centuries

The 12th-century former abbey-church at Souillac is now a sumptuous parish church.

cave — the Painted Gallery and the Bull Chamber. You go in through a museum showing the story of the cave which was occupied about 15,000 years BC.

In the caves are engravings of bisons pierced by arrows, herds of deer, horses, something strangely like a unicorn, and a remarkable great black bull. The nearest to a man has a man's body and a bird's head. All sorts of theories have been suggested about this being a sanctuary dedicated to primitive rites or a place of magic cults, but it might have been just a well-decorated home. It is an interesting mystery but not at all important: what is magical is to think that people lived here so long ago. Certainly, the colours were remarkably clear when the discovery was made, and some drawings are superimposed on others, suggesting that the walls were decorated through several generations.

Southwards 5km just before Thonac is a delightfully elegant Renaissance château on the edge of the river — **Château de Losse**. Built in 1576, it contains superb Louis XIII furniture and tapestries (tours 1st July to 15th September).

From Montignac take the little road on the east bank of the Vézère through Aubas and Condat-sur-Vézère for lovely views. **Aubas** has a Louis XIII château, de Sauveboeuf, and a church with beautiful 16th-century capitals with interlaced figures.

Condat, at the meeting place of the Vézère and Coly rivers, has picturesque buildings of the ancient Knights Hospitallers including the church, fortified living quarters flanked by square towers and houses with high roofs and towers. There is a clutch of local châteaux, too — Château la Petite Filoloe (17th-century manor), Châteaux des Peyraux (over N89 — restored in the 18th century and flanked by round towers) and la Fleunie (16th–17th centuries). Alas, Condat's local industry is now paper-making, and sometimes there is a smell like cooking cauliflower in the air, which is bad luck indeed for the pleasant little inn, the Sautet — alongside at Le Lardin–St. Lazare on the N89 — which serves excellent traditional Périgourdine dishes of goose and duck (no cauliflower).

Westward from Le Lardin along N89 you come to **La Bachellerie**, whose church stands in ruins as the English left it in the Hundred Years' War in the 14th century. Just past it is **Château de Rastignac**, built around 1812 by a local architect, Blanchard. It looks surprisingly like the White House in Washington and the rumour has spread that the White House was based on it. But the houses based on the style of the great Palladio abounded at that time, all over Europe and beyond. Rastignac was burned down by the Germans in 1945 — one of those thousands of pointless acts of vandalism performed by the Nazis when they were retreating and knew that they had lost. It has been rebuilt. You cannot visit it but you can drive along the superb tree-lined avenue leading to it to get a better look.

From Condat take the lovely tiny road through a valley with wooded slopes south of the Vézère to the delightful busy little market town of **Terrasson**, astride the Vézère, unnoticed by so many motorists hurrying along the N89 above it. The old town is on one side of the river, the 'new' town on the other, joined by a modern bridge and a medieval bridge from the 12th century. The old part rises from a 12th-century port in terraces up the hillside to the 15th-century church. From the church terrace you can see over the slate roofs of the houses which run higgledy-piggledy down to the river, with views of the countryside beyond. The ramparts of the ruined fort are terraced into steps. The river is lined with poplars and walnut plantations, and at Terrasson's Thursday market buyers come from hundreds of kilometres in season to buy walnuts and truffles.

A delightful route from Terrasson to Larche, on the border of Corrèze, is to take D63 to Chavagnac, which has a 12th-century church with cupola, then D60 which crosses and re-crosses the Corrèze border within 7km. **Larche** has a village inn, La Bacière, serving excellent cheap meals. 5km south is the pleasant Lac de Causse.

The countryside, hamlets and little lanes south of Terrasson and Larche are delightful down to Souillac, whether in Corrèze, Périgord or Lot. You can easily get lost and to do so is most rewarding. But first you may want to look at **Brive-la-Gaillarde**, a lively, welcoming and useful town on the Corrèze river. It is very busy, has an important railway station where Motorail trains unload cars and people from Calais on their way to holidays in the Dordogne, some good value restaurants and a few fine old buildings. Best of these is Hôtel de Labenche, a superb piece of Renaissance architecture in yellow stone. It is a library and not open but you can enter the courtyard and see the great arched arcades and the beauty of the decoration.

Two museums are interesting — Musée Ernest-Rupin, in a Louis XIII mansion, with items from prehistoric to Gothic, and Napoléonic furniture donated by Lord Campbell, one of Napoléon's guards on Elba, and the Edmond Michelet Museum in rue Champanatier, devoted to the story of the French Resistance in World War II, deportation to Germany and concentration camps, especilly Dachau where Michelet was a prisoner.

Brive is a centre for a fruit and market gardening area and its excellent Saturday market, outside the much-restored 13th-century church of St. Martin, offers temptations from all over Périgord as well as local fruit and vegetables.

A lovely road (D38) takes you through wooded hills and valleys, walnuts and vines to the medieval city of **Collonges-la-Rouge** (see box). From Larche, a very pretty little road (D19) winds through hills, hamlets and past farms to the N20. You pass a lake at **Chasteaux** where you can swim. Even the N20 soon runs into lovely country at Cressensac as it crosses into the Lot.

Souillac, where the busy N20 crosses the Dordogne, is the centre for shopping, banks and main market for a huge area. And in mid-summer, when campers, caravanners and holiday-makers from gîtes converge on it, it can be desperately crowded, with queues for banks, and tables in restaurants and cafés hard to come by. But it is amusing if you don't mind being jostled a bit. The town grew up around a 13th-century abbey, destroyed by the English and then again in the Wars of Religion in 1572. The abbey church has survived and is a gem — Romanesque Byzantine, with three deep domes. The curving lines of its roof are beautiful. The uncluttered, harmonious single nave is light and spacious and contains an old doorway which is a fine piece of Romanesque sculpture, carved with

intricate beauty. A bas-relief above the door tells the story of St. Theophilus. A monk, he was removed from his job as Deacon of the monastery of Adana by a new abbot. He was so cross that he signed a pact with the Devil to help him get his job back. Relenting, he prayed to the Virgin Mary for forgiveness and she appeared to him in his sleep to show him that she had expunged his name from the contract and obtained his pardon. Faustus could have done with a dream like that.

For centuries the people of Souillac ran boats on the Dordogne, taking vine stakes, barrel staves, wine, corn and even cattle to Bordeaux. Laden with salt, they returned upstream pulled by oxen. (See pp. 95–100 for other places such as Martel and La Treyne within short range of Souillac.)

A pleasant way back to Le Lardin from Souillac is by D15, then D62 to the sleepy village of Borrèze, where the road climbs to the junction with D60. Two kilometres left is the Château of **Salignac–Eyvigues**. A medieval fortress from the 12th century, surrounded by ramparts, it still belongs to the family from which came the great Fénelon, 17th-century writer, cleric, and finally Archbishop of Cambrai. The castle is flanked by round and square towers, with mullioned windows in the central building. At the top of a Renaissance spiral staircase are rooms with attractive Renaissance and Louis XIII furniture. The cellars have two levels. There are guided tours in season. There is a covered market in Salignac square.

Turn right on D60, then left on D62 to **La Cassagne**, a typical Périgord village set around a lovely Romanesque church. Here is a little distillery producing liqueurs and a famous walnut apéritif. D62 continues to Le Lardin.

Hotels and Restaurants

A = very expensive, B = expensive, C = moderately expensive, D = moderate, E = inexpensive.

BOURDEILLES — 24310 Brantôme. Griffons, le pont (53.03.75.61). 16th-century beside 13th-century river bridge. Meals C–D; rooms D–E. Closed 15 Oct–1 May.

BRANTÔME — 24310 Dordogne. Moulin de l'Abbeye, route de Bourdeilles (53.05.80.22). Romantic watermill. Fine Périgourdian dishes. Meals A–B; rooms A–B. Closed early Nov–end April.
Chabrol, 5 rue Gambetta (53.05.70.15). By river bridge. Jean-Claude Charbonnel has a passion for cooking. Meals A–D; rooms D. Closed 15 Nov–15 Dec.
Auberge du Soir, 6 rue Georges Saumande (53.05.82.93). 18th-century *auberge rurale*. Good value. Meals C–E; rooms E.

BRIVE-LA-GAILLARDE—19100 Corrèze. La Crémaillère, 53 av Paris (55.74.32.47). Try stuffed goose neck, cassoulet with goose confit. Meals C–E; rooms D–E.
La Périgourdine, 15 av Alsace–Lorraine (55.24.26.55). Charming restaurant with garden; good value. Meals B–E.

CHAMPAGNAC-DE-BELAIR — 24530 Dordogne. Moulin du Roc (53.54.80.36). Beautifully converted watermill by Dronne river. Solange Gardillou is probably France's best woman chef. Meals A–B; rooms B–C. Closed 15 Nov–15 Dec; 15 Jan–mid March.

COLLONGES-LA-ROUGE — 19500 Corrèze. Auberge le Prieuré (55.25.41.00). Good bargain menus; regional dishes. Meals E; rooms E.
Relais St. Jacques de Compostelle (55.25.41.02). Attractive; good variety of dishes. Meals B–E; rooms E. Closed mid Jan–mid March.

CRESSENSAC — 46600 Martel Chez Gilles, on M20 (65.37.70.06). Logis. Good value meals. Meals C–E; rooms D–E.

EXCIDEUIL — 24160 Dordogne. Fin Chapon, pl Château (53.62.42.38). Founded 1750. Périgourdian specialties. Meals C–E; rooms E.

LARCHE — 19600 Corrèze. La Bacière (55.85.30.04). Jean-Phillipe Marcou serves remarkable value meals, old style. Meals D–E.

MONTIGNAC — 24290 Dordogne. Château du Puy Robert, 1.5-km by D65 (53.51.92.13). Manor in park; beautifully decorated inside; luxurious and pricy. Meals A–C; rooms A. Closed mid Oct–early May.

PÉRIGUEUX — 24000 Dordogne. L'Oison, 31 rue St. Front (53.09.84.02). Some of the best regional cooking in Périgord, by Régis Chiorozas. Meals B–D.
Périgord, 74 rue Victor-Hugo (53.53.33.63). Old favourite. Pleasant rooms. Nice garden. Excellent regional dishes. Meals D–E; rooms E.

SORGES — 24420 Savignac-Les-Eglises. Auberge de la Truffe, on N21 (53.05.02.05). Pleasant inn, outstanding Périgourdine dishes. Meals C–E; rooms C–E. Pool.

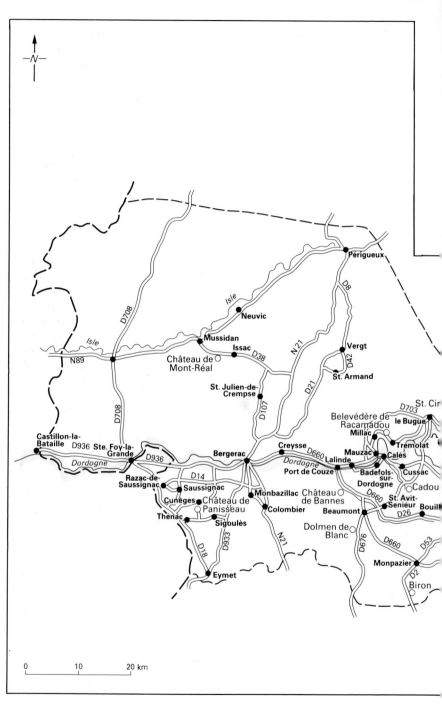

5
Bergerac to Sarlat

Bergerac

Bergerac is a town with two faces. Those passing through on N21 to or from Périgueux and the south see a rather scruffy, slightly forlorn town of 1930s style industrialism, a place which has seen better days. But those who wander around, go to the market, explore the old town, eat and drink there, soon have great affection for it. To judge it from the N21 is like judging somewhere from a railway line.

True, its tobacco factory and Musée de Tabac seem obsolete these days, and the main unglamorous product is nitro-cellulose for paint, plastics and films. But, above all, it is still a wine town. It was known for wine in the Middle Ages, once threatened Bordeaux for supremacy, went through a wine-slump until recently and now its wine has improved beyond belief and its wine business is again booming. Furthermore, it remains the market and marketing town for the vineyards, farms producing peaches, pears and apples for a whole area along and around the Dordogne river. It is very much a living country town.

Though N21 is the shortest route from Périgueux to Bergerac, a more pleasant route is to branch off N21 on to D8 to Vergt, after which it becomes the D21 running beside the little Caudau river.

Vergt has become the most important strawberry market in France and during the season, from late April to the end of October, they are sold by the tonne in the Friday market. It is an important chicken market, too. Around here at St. Armand, a few kilometres south, is a popular camping area, and good fishing.

The Dordogne département stretches much farther west from Périgueux and down to Bergerac than most people realise. This area of Forêt de la Double and Forêt du Landais gets scant mention even in the Michelin Green Guide and is ignored totally by nearly all British guides. Nor do many realise that a quarter of the Dordogne is still forest.

Double is still the wildest part of the Dordogne with few buildings. It stretches from Périgueux south to the N89 and west to the Gironde border north-east of St. Emilion. It was always a forest land of huge oaks, chestnuts and pines with thick undergrowth, and the clearings were mostly created originally by charcoal burners. Pigs and wood were the means of survival. From the start of the last century trees were felled *en masse* for Napoléon's ships and then for railway sleepers. In the clay soil, water collected in marshes and malaria took hold, so that the few poor people who had been scraping a living in the area, abandoned it.

Napoléon III, who was deeply interested in land reclamation and had set himself up a model farm to reclaim part of the Sologne in the Loire, found the money for a reclamation scheme, and it was handed over to Trappist monks

Vineyards in the grounds of Château de Monbazillac producing luscious white wine

Cyrano de Bergerac

In 1897, Edmond Rostand became famous by writing a sad play in verse called 'Cyrano de Bergerac' about a brilliant swordsman and poet who had such an ugly big nose that he had to fight a thousand duels to defend his honour after insults and who was spurned by every woman for his looks, including the love of his life, the lovely Roxane. Sadly, he wrote love poems to Roxane for a friend to woo her. It was a very-French sad romantic tale, wildly melodramatic. Yet Cyrano de Bergerac *did* live, from 1619 to 1655, was a soldier and swordsman, fought many a duels and was a writer, too. But he was a wit and satirist, and his *Histoire Comique des Etats de la Lune et du Soleil* (Comic History of the States of the Moon and the Sun) was said to have suggested 'Gulliver' to Swift and 'Micromégas' to Voltaire. He was renowned for love letters, too, and was a fighter and adventurer. Born Savinien de Cyrano in Paris, he attended the college at Beauvais, fought in several battles and was twice wounded, the second time ending his military career. He then studied astronomy.

Bergerac named a street after him half a century before the Rostand play was put on, and in modern times has used his face on wine posters, showing his great nose appreciating the great 'nose' of Bergerac red wine. Scholars have tried to tell us recently that he had nothing to do with Bergerac on the Dordogne but with some unknown Bergerac just outside Paris. Why will didactic scholars spoil a good story with too many facts? To any romantic and lover of wine, he belongs in Périgord.

who set up a monastery at Echourgnac. Despite all of them falling victims to malaria fever they drained marshes, planted vines and raised cattle. In 1901 when most religious orders were expelled from France, they were allowed to remain to continue their work. The Trappists are still there, and make a very good cheese, excuse enough for their remaining.

Malaria has gone from Double, so have the vipers, but nearly 60 per cent of it is still woodland, and few people live there. Cattle are raised for meat and dairy products. Two little towns are on the N89 which divides Double forest from the forest of Landais. Neuvic produces shoes. Mussidan, where the rivers Isle and Crempse meet, is a small industrial town specialising in ceramics. It has a reputation for rebellion. The town and people suffered greatly for Protestant sympathies and in 1944 the local Resistance attacked a munitions train and 53 townspeople were killed by the Nazis in reprisal. Eastward, 7km along D38, just before Issac on the river Crempse, is the impressive **Château de Mont-Réal**, on top of a great rock overlooking the river. It still has some of its 11th-century double ramparts. Like so many in the Dordogne, it is two châteaux in one. There is a solid and bulky medieval fortress with curtain walls and round tower and a Renaissance 'house' with pretty windows, columns and decorative medallions. A spiral staircase in a tower leads to a fine family chapel containing stone statues, and the 15th-century tomb of François de Pontbriand and his three wives.

Mont-Réal gave its name to the great Canadian city Montreal. Claude de Pontbriand, who sailed with Jacques Cartier, thought that the St. Lawrence river rivalled the Crempse!

Landais forest is not so wild as Double but is heavily wooded. Maritime vines are replacing chestnuts, alas, but there are fruit orchards and tobacco fields, too.

Westward, 22km from Bergerac, right on the Dordogne river on D936, is **Ste. Foy-la-Grande**, an ancient bastide — medieval new towns usually fortified for defence (see box. p. 10). This one was built by Louis IX's third brother Alphonse de Poitiers, who built nearly as many of them as did Edward I of England. But the English took it when Alphonse died of the plague in 1271 and his property reverted to Aquitaine, which was under English rule through Henry II of England's marriage to Eleanor of Aquitaine. Ste. Foy changed hands several times, until the French took it when the English were driven out of this part of France. But its troubles started all over again in the Wars of Religion when Catholic Leaguers and Protestants fought over it. Somehow, many of its fine medieval houses have survived. This was a centre, too, of Resistance to the Nazis, particularly the smaller town of St. Antoine de Breuilh, where, soon after France's surrender, the people organised a spy system sending information to London about German ships in Bordeaux harbour.

The Dordogne département ends along this D936 just 15km before St. Emilion at Castillon-la-Bataille. Here, too, in July 1453, ended the English rule in South-West France (see p. 13).

Bergerac strides the Dordogne river where it is deep, which made it an important inland port and a place of strategic importance, for the river was bridged here. Its fine main bridge makes it still the most important crossing point of the Dordogne and the most important town in southern Dordogne, as Périgueux is of northern Dordogne. These towns have always been rivals and especially so since the Religious Wars, when Bergerac was staunchly Protestant, Périgueux ardently Catholic. To defend themselves from the Catholic League troops, the people of Bergerac rebuilt their ramparts from stone gathered by knocking down Catholic convents. Inevitably, it was Richelieu who later removed the ramparts. When the Edict of Nantes was revoked, Protestantism became illegal and Protestants were appallingly persecuted. At least half of the people of Bergerac fled to England or Holland, and the prosperous commercial town nearly died. Happily one convent, des Récollets, survived and it is fitting that this should now be the Maison du Vin, headquarters of the Winemakers' Guild. You can visit it and see the vast wine cellar with splendid vaulting and the ornate great hall on the first floor with views of the Monbazillac vineyards.

Bordeaux was Bergerac's other enemy. The Bordelais for centuries pulled every trick to corner wine exports from the Gironde and Dordogne, trying to stop Bergerac selling wine outside its own area. The people of Périgord fought as hard to avoid sending their wine through Bordeaux, shipping it through Bergerac and Libourne. The Bordelais were mostly successful, clamping taxes on all their rivals' wines and even fiddling barrel sizes, until in 1520 Francis I imposed free trade. But as ships became bigger Bordeaux was certain to win, and the English love of what they called 'claret' from Bordeaux meant that much of the Bergerac wine went to Holland. But Bergerac red wines were highly regarded still at the end of the last century, and after a period of mediocrity have improved enormously under modern methods. Both white and red are fast gaining in popularity and esteem.

The old port from which the wines were shipped is still there, as also in the old quarter to the north are medieval and Renaissance houses in narrow streets, and covered market. On Wednesday and Friday farmers sell direct to the public in the shadow of Notre Dame church.

As befits a Périgourdine town, it has good restaurants, with Le Cyrano in boulevard Montaigne offering the best meals at surprisingly reasonable prices, especially during the week. Regional dishes excel.

A popular flea market is held in Bergerac on the first Sunday in each month. At St. Julien-de-Crempse, northward 12km by N21 and D107 left, is a lovely Louis XIV manor house, called Manoir de Grand Vignoble, which has been converted into a luxurious hotel in a park with a pool and stables.

To the east of the N21, in the gravelly hills north-east of Bergerac, the best red Pécharmant wines are produced. These and some of the Réserve wines from top producers around Monbazillac are the best of the Bergerac reds. Grape varieties are limited to Cabernet Sauvignon, Cabernet Franc, Merlot and Malbec, and the

Château de la Jaubertie, Colombier, the Ryman home, was probaly built by Henry of Navarre for his mistress, Gabrielle d'Estrées, then altered in Napoleonic times as a love-nest for a dancer and doctor.

53

Ryman Wine

Nicholas Ryman sold his stationer's empire in England before he was 40 to achieve his ambition to make wine in France. He bought the charming but run-down 16th century Château la Jaubertie at Colombier, 8km from Bergerac, along with its rather run-down vineyards and started without knowing anything! Within a few years his wine was recognised by French experts such as Patrick Dusset-Garber (adviser to the French trade) as the Bergerac to buy. At the great Macon Wine Fair, his white wine won silver and bronze medals, his red wine two golds. He found that Bergerac red producers were using oak barrels up to 100 years old, resulting in so much tannin that not even ten years of maturing could soften it. Nicholas used the Bordeaux method of introducing a high percentage of new casks every year. Kept five or six years, the Jaubertie Reserve red is superb — fruity, mouth-filling and well structured.

Meanwhile his son Hugh studied wine at Bordeaux University's famous wine school and in Australia at Petaluma under Brian Croser, widely called the best white wine maker in the world. Back at Jaubertie, Hugh made delicious white wines — a fruity and refreshing Bergerac dry white made mainly from Sémillon grapes and an extra fruity, perfumed Sauvignon Bergerac with about 20 per cent Sémillon. Then Hugh set off to conquer the white wine world. With his team of winemakers, mostly Australian, he made wine the modern way for many growers in Bergerac, South-West France, the Duras, Hungary, Slovakia, Bulgaria and the former Soviet state of Moldavia. He is now one of the greatest white wine makers in Europe. His name on the back label of a bottle means that the wine is around the top of its class.

In 1994 Nicholas Ryman decided to retire. We all feared for Jaubertie. Would it fall to a multi-national group and become just a brand name? But Hugh moved in. He formed a partnership with another English wine-maker, Esme Johnstone, who makes a distinguished red Bordeaux wine at the 17th century Château de Sours in the Gironde. They run Jaubertie — Hugh makes the wine and Esme manages the administration — and Nicholas Ryman still lives in the Château.

---

minimum alcohol is 11 per cent, though most are stronger. They are rich in colour, almost purple when young, meaty and generous, and go well with *charcuterie*, red meat, game and cheese, served at room temperature (18°C). The best are kept a year to 18 months in the wood and then in bottle until six years old, though they will last until ten. They need time to get rid of excess tannin from their long stay in the wood and they become full-bodied and beautifully balanced.

The flag carrier from the last century of Pécharmant was **Château de Tire-gand**. This beautiful and huge château, built in 1688, is reached by taking D660 from Bergerac towards Lalinde. When a board marking the village of Creysse appears, turn left under the railway bridge and the château is on the left. The owners and wine producers are the Comte and Comtesse of St. Exupéry, cousins of the airman–poet Antoine de St. Exupéry, who was killed in the Second World War. You can taste the wine here and buy it. For other Bergerac wine tastings, see the Wine Tastings box on p. 22.

Bergerac's red wines with an Appellation Contrôlée (AOC) rating are descendants of those which challenged Bordeaux red last century and which were often passed off as Bordeaux until more recent times. They are permitted exactly the same grape types as Pécharmant, which is exactly the same as Bordeaux red, but plus a local grape called Fer, of which we found that some local people have never heard. It gives a dark colour and 'rustic' taste. Most wines are lighter than Bordeaux, have more fruit, and are drunk between one and four years. Some wines, from the hills around Monbazillac, are fuller-bodied, deeper in colour and more tannic when young, and mature into very attractive wines after four to six years. Bergerac rosés are refreshing but not outstanding.

It is Bergerac white wine which has improved so much over recent years — *some* of the white, anyway. White Bergerac used to be slightly sweet — demi-sec. Now wines are dry, crisp, fruity and the best are beautifully perfumed. Grape varieties used are Sémillon, which makes the wine softer, gives flavour and richness, Sauvignon, which is very fruity and gives body, and Muscadelle, which gives the rich, musky bouquet, plus a little Ondec and Chenin Blanc, used extensively in the Loire. More Sauvignon is being used these days, making the wines drier, and one or two of the best producers are producing also a Sauvignon wine which is extra perfumed because it is mixed with some Sémillon.

Some of the very best whites are produced in Saussignac (Côtes de Saussignac — at least 12.5 per cent alcohol, very mouth-filling and delightful with *charcuterie*, fish and white meats).

Monbazillac wine from the village 7km south of Bergerac is sweet, white and greatly underestimated, though enjoying a well-deserved comeback. It is made from the same grape varieties as Sauternes and was for long passed-off as Sauternes, though in good years it is richer. The grape varieties are Sémillon, Sauvignon and a little Muscadelle. As with Sauternes, the grapes are picked in late autumn when they have been affected by the 'Noble Rot' (Pourriture noble or botrytis) which makes them shrivel and gives them so much sugar. The minimum strength is 13 per cent of alcohol but most wines are much stronger.

Young, the wine is straw-coloured and honeyed and makes a good apéritif drunk very cold, or it can be drunk with foie gras, liver pâté or any fruit dessert. But it is best kept at least five years, preferably ten, when it is amber-coloured and luscious. Serve it very cold with those lovely strawberries from Vergt. It is also used for making a pricy crayfish soup.

To reach **Monbazillac**, take the pretty D13 road south from Bergerac, between D933 and N21. You climb up to a medieval hamlet among vineyards and you reach the *Château de Monbazillac*, which is very beautiful, with round towers at each corner and an attractive courtyard. Built in 1550 for pleasure as well as defence, it became a Protestant stronghold in the Wars of Religion and contains a museum of Protestantism which includes early bibles and prayer books, many printed in Holland. The Dutch had a taste for sweet Monbazillac wine. But now the château is owned by the Co-operative of Monbazillac wine producers, who have restored it, and it has a few superb fireplaces and tapestries. More important, its enormous cellars, running the

View over the Dordogne from the spectacular corniche — Cingle de Trémolat

full length and breadth of the building, are laid out as a museum of wine, with old bottles and wine-making equipment. In a converted barn, in the courtyard, you can taste wine and buy it, and in season there is a restaurant open in the courtyard. From the château terraces are fine views across the vineyards to Bergerac. And right by the walls in this tiny village is a superb restaurant, la Closerie St. Jacques, in an ancient pilgrims' relais, serving Périgourdine dishes and fine local wines. Cheaper menus are good value and

it serves a good lower-priced lunch.

The caves of the Co-operative are on the right along D933 from Bergerac or you can reach them by the tiny D14 from the Château. You can taste and buy wines from the cave Monday–Friday. Very modern methods of vinification are used and they produce Monbazillacs of their own vineyards, Pécharmant from Château la Renaudie and Bergerac white, red and rosé.

But before going to the cave, continue from the Château on little marked white roads in the hills to Colombier

Montaigne

The man who invented the literary word and form which we call Essays was Michel Eyquem de Montaigne, born at the Château de Montaigne near Montcaret at the western end of Périgord in 1533. He called his first book of comments on life and literature 'Essaies', meaning attempts or experiments. He was an original thinker, subjecting everything he experienced or read to fearless, all-questioning criticism, though using it in an almost-casual style of writing.

His great-grandfather, a Bordeaux wine-merchant called Ramon Eyquem, bought the Montaigne château at St. Michel-de-Montaigne, so buying the family into the aristocracy. Michel had an extraordinary upbringing. Though his father made him mix on equal terms with villagers and boys from the castle estate, he employed a tutor to teach him Latin until he was six, and at home he was allowed to speak or hear nothing but Latin. Even the servants were taught to speak to him in Latin. Then he went to the College of Guyenne at Bordeaux where he was taught by the Scottish humanist, George Buchanan; it must have come as something of a shock to the boy to be taught by a Scot speaking French. And he admitted later that he knew not a word of French until he was six!

He then studied law at the University of Toulouse and returned to Bordeaux at 21 to practise at the Bordeaux bar, which he hated. When he was 35 his father died and left him the Montaigne estate, so he was able to live the life of a country gentleman. He wrote and published his books of Essays and other works.

Like his father, he was elected Mayor of Bordeaux, against his wishes. Times were difficult — plague and pestilence were sweeping Europe and the Religious Wars were on. Half the population of Bordeaux died of the plague. Though a Catholic and loyal to Charles IX, he was a friend of the Protestant leader Henry of Navarre, who came to stay with him, and he tried to bring the extreme-Catholic Leaguers and the Protestants together, so receiving the wrath of both. He fled with his household when the plague reached his village and when he returned his château had been looted by soldiers, but was still habitable. He died in bed in 1592. Alas, a disastrous fire burned out his château in 1855, and all that is left is the tower where he wrote.

Montaigne's philosophy of life was one which contradicted all the modern theories of competition and striving for success. To live, he said, was in itself the most fundamental and marvellous of all occupations. The true aim of life, he wrote, is not to win or to write books or to gain battles and lands and property, but to live an orderly and tranquil life. 'To live properly is our great and glorious masterpiece.'

A constant advocate of tolerance, he pointed out that no two men ever had the same opinion of the same thing. He is still extremely readable, and his sense of humour shines through. Perhaps the strongest opinions he held were on smells. He disliked the smell of Paris but loved the smell of good food, as befits a man of Périgord.

hamlet and Château la Jaubertie, a charming 16th-century château which it is believed that Henry of Navarre (later Henry IV of France), who loved women, wine, food and life, gave to his mistress Gabrielle d'Estrées then was a dancer and doctor's love nest. It is a delightful house, and although you cannot enter because it is still the home of Nicholas Ryman, you can see it very well through the open gateway. And in a little tasting room by the caves outside the gate you can taste and buy the best white Bergerac and Sauvignon made in the area (see box, p. 54).

This is a very rewarding area for travellers who want to discover good new French country wines. Westward from the D933, or just south of the D936 westward from Bergerac, is **Saussignac**, which has an old château where the beautiful hostess Louise de la Beraudière, wife of Louis d'Estissac, used to entertain such literatary figures as the great scholar, gourmet and wit, Rabelais, who had been her husband's tutor, the satirist Brantôme, and Montaigne, the great essayist who was born and lived near Montcaret, just north of D936 at the west end of Périgord (see box). Opposite the château at Saussignac is the pleasant Hôtel de Saussignac taken over recently by a very talented young chef, Thierry Descard, from la Corniche, Rolleboise — excellent value. At the nearby village of **Razac-de-Saussignac**, Pierre-Jean

Sardoux, renowned oenologist from the Institute of Bordeaux, uses modern equipment, including a laboratory, to make Court Les Mûts, the best of Saussignac wines. Made from old vines, 40 per cent Merlot, the red wine matures for 18 months in *new* oak barrels (like the best Bordeaux) and will keep 6–7 years, when the tannin becomes softened and the wine beautifully full. The white, 70 per cent Sémillon, is a delight. You can taste and buy.

It is worth finding **Château de Panisseau** not only for its wine-tasting but for the delightful 13th-century château. In 1363 when the English owned Aquitaine, the Seigneur de Panisseau paid homage for his title to the Prince of Wales — the great warrior Black Prince, who was also Prince of Aquitaine. You will see Panisseau marked on the yellow Michelin map just north of the tiny road between Sigoulès and Thénac, west of D933. The red wine from this château has twice won a Mâcon Gold Medal and has a specially long-lasting flavour.

And Thénac is very near to the most attractive little D18 road running from Ste. Roy-la-Grande to Eymet, a bastide on the southern border of the Dordogne département. It is another one built by Alphonse de Poitiers in 1271, badly knocked around in wars but still with many 15th-century houses and a fine market place with arcades and a 17th-century fountain. It is known for its conserves, especially of plums.

Bergerac to les Eyzies

A road which starts drearily past the Bergerac cellulose factory and an

armament depot, out of sight of the Dordogne which is so tantalisingly near

it, takes you towards some of the most beautiful country in this whole area of France, some of the most interesting sights, and can point you to hideaways where few tourists are seen and the fields and woods still provide the main livelihood of the villages.

The D660 runs on the north bank of the Dordogne river to Port de Couze, just before Lalinde, then crosses the river and becomes much less important and more interesting. At Port de Couze there are so many attractive alternative routes that quite the best thing to do is to stay in one of the villages or little towns farther east or south-east, explore all the routes and get lost as well to discover little gems of hamlets. A week would be the minimum to stay. This is a splendid area to hire a gîte for a fortnight or more.

Once over the river the D660 is very appealing as far as Beaumont-du-Périgord, a bastide built for the English King Edward I in 1272, and pleasant as far as the delightful bastide of Monpazier. From there the equally appealing D53 takes you to the superb hilltop town of Belvès. (More about all these later.) Just before Beaumont you can turn left off D660 on another lovely winding road D26 which wanders beside the little Couze river to Bouillac, then to Belvès.

Instead of crossing at Port de Couze, you can take D703 between the Dordogne river and the Lalinde canal to **Lalinde** itself, another old bastide built by the English in 1270 but damaged badly in the Wars of Religion. The Germans finished it off by burning it down in a huff when they were retreating in 1944 and being harassed by the French Resistance fighters. But it is still a lively little commercial and market town, and has a pleasant old hotel, the

'Château', which is in a formidable little 13th-century fortress with pointed turrets. Its terrace for summer eating overhangs the river, with nice views.

At Lalinde you can cross the river on to D29, with excellent riverside views to Badefols-sur-Dordogne, then take another pretty road D28 to the Cistercian Abbey at Cadouin and the winding D25 through woods and very quiet countryside to Le Buisson, where you can cross the river again on to the road to Le Bugue.

The D703 from Lalinde and the D31 to Mauzac take you on one of the most spectacular and rewarding drives in the whole of this part of France — The **Cingle de Trémolat**. The Dordogne here takes two enormous great loops and the little road which climbs up from Mauzac winds through woods above the white cliffs of the river to give superb views of the river below, lined with poplars and crossed by bridges of golden stone. Cingle means 'meander' and that is just what the Dordogne is doing. The best view is from the Belvédère de Racamadou. From a platform by the water tower you have a superb panorama of the river and countryside. There is a splendid view, too, from the terrace of the Panoramic Hôtel, where regional dishes are good value.

Beneath the cliffs the river snakes through pretty country. A watersports centre has been set up for yachting, canoeing, rowing, with regattas in summer, and swimming.

Trémolat village is so charmingly French that Claude Chabrol chose it as the typical French village for his film *Le Boucher* — a rather sinister story. But there is certainly nothing sinister about the big old Mairie, with the village school in its wings and children playing on its terrace shaded by pollarded

The garden of Le Vieux Logis, the country hotel at Trémolat, is as charming as its furnishings and food

plane trees. The local inn, unspoiled by time or tourists, is still family run and serves really cheap meals. The little old village houses in winding lanes look warm and friendly and purely Péri-gourdian.

The old church, mind you, is a bit cold, sinister and strange. Built by Benedictines in the 12th century on the foundations of an earlier church built on the orders of Charlemagne, it is a fort with a bell-tower, and looks like an old warehouse. Inside is a single nave of

four bays, one of which has walls 2m thick from the earlier church. This is a fine example of the fortified village churches of the 12th century when they were the only defence against armed marauding bands or passing looting armies. Even the bell-tower is a keep in disguise, and the church could have held every soul in the village in an emergency. It measures 350 square metres. What is surprising is that no passing warlord or destructive band of soldiery knocked it down, not even the

Limeuil — old hillside village where the Dordogne meets the Vézère

English or the contestants in the Wars of Religion. Time and weather left their mark, but some restoration has been done. The small Romanesque Chapelle St. Hilaire in the cemetery has been excellently restored. This is where church services are held now for the villagers. The fortified church is damp, dark, gloomy and impossible to heat. The chapel has fine modern stained-glass windows by Paul Becker. It is fitting that one should show a fish, for you will see many fishermen alongside the Dordogne here.

The greatest joy for us in Trémolat is the village Logis. Le Vieux Logis is far from being a snug Logis de France these days. It is a Relais et Châteaux hotel, and is expensive, but it is sheer delight and worth every franc it costs to stay or eat there. Bernard Giraudel gives it the same loving care as his mother did. All the bedrooms are different, all furnished in old style, though a few are in converted stables. Jean-Pierre Duribreux is a true classic chef, and we have never had a bad dish, from peasant omelette to confit of duck. Better book (53.22.80.06).

The D31 to Le Bugue passes almost over the rooftops of another gem on the Dordogne river, **Limeuil**. At this beauty spot the river Vézère joins the Dordogne, with the lovely Pont Coude (Elbow Bridge) spanning both rivers. The tightly packed old houses of the little town are in winding streets up the cliffside and from the esplanade of the old castle the panorama is impressive. It is now a place for fishing, canoeing and swimming, and the riverside quay can get packed with cars in mid-summer. Once it was a heavily fortified town and there are still remains of its ramparts and three gates. The restored domed

church of St. Martin was built in 1194 during English occupation. Richard Coeur de Lion was one of its founders and it was originally dedicated to St. Thomas à Becket, murdered by the knights of Richard's father Henry II at Canterbury Cathedral. Limeuil was a centre of fighting during the Wars of Religion when it belonged to the Protestant Viscount of Turenne, father of the famous Turenne who played such a part in the military history of France in the 17th century. Another of its well-known inhabitants was Isabeau de Limeuil, one of Catherine de Médicis' team of attractive seductresses. She became mistress of the Prince of Condé. Later, the town was a centre of weaving and boat building.

Le Bugue, 6km along D31, is one of those small towns which motorists tend to drive through, maybe cursing the traffic on market days, or in which they stop just for a cup of coffee or snack. In fact it is a lively agreeable little town on the Vézère and convenient as a touring centre. The meeting place of the Vézère and Dordogne is nearby, there are facilities for watersports and good camp sites. Le Bugue has Renaissance houses with iron balconies and it holds two markets a week on Tuesday and Saturday mornings, a fair on the third Tuesday of every month and two main old-style Dordogne fairs on 25th August and 30th September.

It has two local caves, too. **Bara-Bahau** cave 2km from town was discovered only in 1951. Created by an underground river, it is 120km long, with engravings made about 20,000 years ago of horses, oxen, bison and rhinoceros, but they are difficult to decipher. **Gouffre de Proumeyssac**, $3\frac{1}{2}$ km south, has fine stalagmites and stalactites, and a stream running through it.

Both caves are open from Palm Sunday to 30th September.

Little roads north of the Dordogne take you to the really spectacular caves of **Les Eyzies** (see box).

Ten kilometres south of Le Bugue is a Dordogne river bridge to **Le Buisson**, a pleasant little place with good cheap restaurants and beaches on the river for swimming. The eastwards arm of the confusing D25 road, by the river, takes you to **Siorac-en-Périgord**, which has a vast 17th-century château with two wings at right angles, one occupied by the town hall. Something of a centre for tourist shopping, it has a market on Wednesdays. An attractive route from here is by D50 across the little river Nauze, following the Dordogne, then D53 to Castelnaud. The southward road D710 from Siorac reaches Belvès in 4km.

Belvès is spectacular in its small way. Climbing from the D710 with valley views, you come suddenly into a square lined with old shops and containing an old covered market dating from the 15th century and a chain attached to a pillar where poor wretches were flogged or pilloried for some minor misdemeanour in the Middle Ages. You climb a little higher between Gothic and Renaissance buildings, many now shops, to another square, place de la Croix-des-Frères, with a former Dominican monastery topped by an octagonal clock tower. Opposite the monastery is a typical old Dordogne inn — little changed for over a century or so and offering good cheap old-style meals. Walk along the top road by the old ramparts and you have splendid views of the countryside over old houses with turrets and bell-towers and terraced gardens.

This is walnut country. About 8km south-east at Doissat is a huge plantation covering 66 hectares set up by a big banker in 1959. At Belvès important walnut sales are held in season at the Saturday market by the old market hall. Walnuts have been a major crop of Périgord for many centuries for eating, for oil and for furniture making (see p. 19).

A delightful road runs from Belvès to Monpazier (see below, p. 68).

The whole area south of the Dordogne river, west of a line from Le Buisson to Belvès, across to Monpazier and up to Beaumont and Lalinde is beautiful, with woods, hills, little rivers and sparsely populated hamlets where people live the old-style life of Périgourdian farmers, which has disappeared from some areas. You meet very few holidaymakers except a few Britons and Dutch staying in the rare gîtes. Even near to the Dordogne river there are little roads which lead to one farm, to a little hamlet such as Cussac where ancient houses are still lived in, or just to woods where you can hide for a day, walking, eating a picnic or reading and meeting nobody but a passing farm worker.

A zig-zagging road from Le Buisson goes to **Cadouin** and its well-restored Cistercian abbey, founded in 1115. Two years later the monks had a lot of luck. They were presented with some ancient cloth said to have been the shroud in which Christ's head was wrapped. It was found hidden in the wall of a church at Antioch and given to the abbey by the Bishop of Puy. The pilgrims came; the abbey became rich and important in the Middle Ages. Men like Richard Coeur de Lion, Louis IX (St. Louis), the crusading King of France, and Charles V came to kneel before it.

During the Hundred Years' War the monks panicked when the English were around and sent their holy shroud for safe keeping to Toulouse and then Aubazines. It took them many lawsuits and the help of Louis XI and a pope to get it back. Then in 1932 experts proved that the Arab inscriptions with which it was decorated were no older than the 11th century. Meanwhile the monks had been expelled during the Revolution.

The façade of the church is massive and austere. It is divided into three by buttresses, is well proportioned and the golden-yellow colour of its stone is enhanced by its simplicity. Inside it is rather gloomy compared with many of the splendid Renaissance churches with their richly coloured glass, but it is authentic Middle Ages, little changed. The central aisle and two apses are all topped by domes, in the Byzantine style similar to Périgueux cathedral. But the cloisters are flamboyantly splendid. They were built with the help of money given by Louis XI after the previous cloisters had been destroyed in the Hundred Years' War and were not finished until the 16th century, so there are some fine Renaissance touches and sculptured decoration on the monks' and abbot's stone seats and on the wall alongside, which has a remarkable fresco showing the Annunciation. Happily, these delightful cloisters, complete with their garden, were not badly damaged in the Revolution and the State bought the abbey and restored it well in the last century. The cloisters are open daily except for 15th December to 31st January, and Tuesdays in winter. They are certainly worth seeing.

The other attractive route to Cadouin is by D29 along the south bank

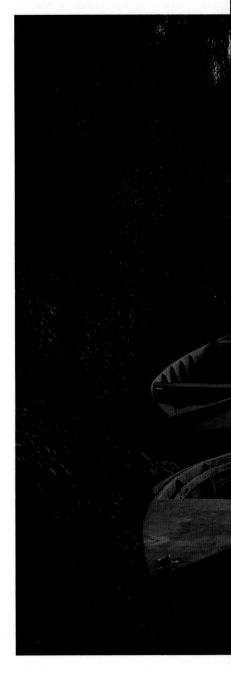

Dusk over the Dordogne at Badefols-sur-Dordogne in late summer

Les Eyzies-de-Tayac

About 35,000 years ago, Cro-Magnon man, his wife and child, lying in a cave beside the Vézère river, where it meets the Beune, were laid to rest. They might still be there, resting in peace, if the railway from Périgueux to Agen had not been built and men moving earth in 1868 had not uncovered their skeletons. Close by at La Madeleine, five years earlier, Edouard Lartet and Henry Christy, distinguished archaeological researchers, had found part of a mammoth's tusk, which had been carved and chiselled. So the search was on for prehistoric man. And no one realised just how much would be found and how much knowledge gleaned about our prehistoric ancestors.

It seems that when man was driven south by the second Ice Age, following the herds of reindeer on which he lived, he took a special liking to the Vézère river because of its convenient caves and rock shelters. The river, which now runs alternately between farmland and walls of rock up to 80m high, was then much higher up the cliffs. So many discoveries have been made in the last 120 years that the little village of Les Eyzies-de-Tayac is called the Capital of Prehistory, and in the medieval fortress of Tayac, one of the castles of the old Barons of Beynac, is the National Museum of Prehistory, interesting to the public, who can visit much of it, a paradise to international archaeologists and other scholars, who can get permission to see it all.

To understand and enjoy Eyzies, you must stay at least two days, there are so many different caves and sites to see. If you are seriously interested, a week would not be too long. And there are other things to do. It is a sailing and swimming centre with a camp site and several hotels and restaurants including the Cro-Magnon and the Centenaire offering superb pricy meals.

We cannot hope in this space or with our limited knowledge of prehistory and archaeology to describe the sites in detail: there are excellent guides obtainable on the spot. However, we do list the main caves. The opening times given here are a guide: do check them when you arrive. Where there are guided tours, numbers are limited and you must buy your tickets in the morning.

Grotte de Font-de-Gaume — 500m from Les Eyzies. Cave 120m long with side chambers and more than 200 paintings and engravings of bison, horses, mammoths, and a remarkable great frieze of brown-black bison on white limestone. They were made around 40,000 years ago. Guided tours. Closed Tue, 1st Nov–25th Dec.

Grotte des Combarelles (3km along D47 east of Eyzies) — two caves discovered in 1901 with drawings of nearly 300 animals, some resting, some galloping. Guided tours. Closed Wed, 1st Nov–25th Dec.

Gisement de Laugerie Haute (north-west of Eyzies to left of D47) — scenic spot at the foot of high cliffs where scientific diggings have been going on since 1863, revealing work and art of cavemen over thousands of years. Guided tours. Open July, Aug, or by pre-booking at Grotte-de-Font-de-Gaume.

Basse Laugerie (just before Haute Laugerie on D47) — display of awls, harpoons, needles, engraved stones and bones, arrow heads, flints, pottery and lamps found under loose stones. Closed Jan.

Grotte de la Mouthe (3km south of Eyzies) — first decorated cave to be discovered in the Périgord (1895). Line drawings of animals, some coloured with ochre. Narrow cave, slippery, unlit, and closed indefinitely for restoration.

Grotte de St. Cirq (south-west of Eyzies just off D706) — animal drawings, but best known for drawings of a human figure. Guided tours daily except Fri.

Musée National de Préhistoire (in village, in Tayac castle) — not to be missed. Set up by Denis Peyrony. Fine views from the platform shared with a dubious statue of primitive man. Open daily, except Tue.

Musée de la Spéléologie (off D47 north-west of Les Eyzies) — pot holing museum in chambers cut out of rock, part of the old rock-fortress of Tayac. Open 3rd July–mid Sept.

Grotte du Grand Roc (north-west of Eyzies, left of D47) — nature's art: stalactites and stalagmites. Fine views from steps. Guided tours. Closed Dec, Jan.

Gorges d'Enfer (Gorge of Hell) — just off D47 north-west of Les Eyzies — small valley where animals, those drawn by cavemen, wander in semi-liberty — tigers, bison, red deer, fallow deer, horses, wild boar and moufflons. Imposing rock shelter. Marked forest trails. Open 21st Mar–14th Nov.

Information about all caves and times of opening from Syndicat d'Initiative, pl Mairie (53.06.97.05), open 15th Mar–Oct.

of the Dordogne, with fine river views. **Badefols-sur-Dordogne** is the main village, in a pleasant riverside position with good fishing. The castle was torn down in 1794 by Joseph Lakanal, who was sent to govern the province of Bergerac after the Revolution. He was a hard man and destroyed several châteaux belonging to aristocrats, but no one minded much about Badefols for it was a hideout of thieves and robbers who preyed on the laden gabares, the Dordogne barges which were poled down the river full of goods to Bergerac, Libourne or Bordeaux, then broken up for the use of their wood. The bargees would buy mules and ride home: the gabares could not return upriver.

Just up river, Calès is perched on a cliff with superb river views. In its fine 12th-century Romanesque church is a statue of Notre Dame du Lac, a virgin to which the gabariers (bargees) used to pray for safe journeys. They had reason. They were not only prey to robbers but many were drowned in dangerous parts of the river.

The attractive little D28 to Cadouin follows the small tributary of the Dordogne, the Belingou.

As we have said, the D660 south from Lalinde passes through fine scenery to Beaumont, and if you take the D26 left the scenery is even better, passing alongside the Couze river through tranquil charming countryside to Bouillac, from where you can soon join the D53, also attractive, to Belvès or to Monpazier. D26 passes hard-by the tiny village of St. Avit-Sénieur which has a massive fortified church with two huge 14th-century towers. It all started when a 6th-century hermit built a chapel. The Norsemen destroyed it in the 9th century but Augustinian monks rebuilt it thoroughly enough to withstand an army. The village has pleasant medieval houses.

Beaumont-du-Périgord is a tiny town of great character. An English bastide of 1272, it still has one of its fortified gates from its great defence walls and around its square are arcades of the ancient market hall. Holding a market was an important privilege of bastides, and peasants from far and wide came to buy and sell. Beaumont still has a fair on the second Tuesday of each month.

Although not as complete as Monpazier to the south, Beaumont still retains many interesting bastide features. The massive fortified gate Porte de Luzier still has the grooves of its portcullis and you can see how invaders who got through this gate would have to run down a narrow passage leading to another fortification. All these bastides had a fortified church as a last retreat for the townsfolk. Beaumont's church, built in the 13th

Monpazier — market square of the beautiful bastide town

century, is a good example, though much restored last century. It has four massive towers at the corners, high solid walls and a sentry walk, and its only decoration is around the doorway and a Gothic balcony over it, with a sculpted frieze mixing, rather strangely, four evangelists, the head of Edward I of England and a stag hunt. Beaumont has some fine 15th-century houses and two old-style inns.

The **Château de Bannes**, 5km northwest, dominates the Couze river valley from a rocky spur. An elegant early 16th-century building flanked by great circular towers and pepper-pot roofs, it is approached across a drawbridge over a dry-moat and has some fine decorations. Alas, it is not open to the public. South of Beaumont is **Dolmen de Blank**, a fine prehistoric megalith. Later, Christians turned this primitive memorial into a 'miracle' with a legend that a frightened young girl caught in a storm prayed to the Virgin Mary and the stones miraculously formed themselves into a shelter.

When we last drove into **Monpazier**, one of our favourite little old towns in France, on an autumn day after the tourist season, we were puzzled to find the roads around the delightful old market square full of cars and the square full of people. We had run into a market for *cèpes*, those nutty-flavoured mushrooms so delicious whether cooked in olive oil or used to add flavour to an omelette or any light dish, or cooked the Périgourdine way with bacon and garlic. Some sellers had brought them in big baskets, others a few in a paper bag. The buyers were studying them with the care they show when buying truffles, which are more costly than gold.

Monpazier was built in 1284 for Edward I of England and much of it has hardly changed since then. Even three of the original six gateways, complete with towers, are still there. So are ancient houses. It was built to complete the English defences of Périgord, with Lalinde and Beaumont, and the Lord of the nearby castle of Biron, Pierre de Gontaut, collaborated. But he played both sides in Anglo–French arguments. In the Hundred Years' War it was pillaged by both French and English troops. In the Wars of Religion it was taken by the Protestant leader, Geoffroi de Vivans. Its enemy was Villefranche-du-Périgord, another bastide built by the French, now on the same road D660 to the south-east. The local story is that the people of Monpazier and Villefranche, unknown to each other, decided to raid and loot each other's towns on the same night. They both set off in the darkness, taking different routes. They both duly arrived home laden with loot to find that their own town had been looted, too.

In 1637, shortly after these wars, Monpazier was the centre of the revolt of the Croquants, the poor peasants, many of whom were starving. A weaver called Buffarot led 8,000 rebels, who tore through the countryside plundering castles. Their major weapon was a bent pitchfork, a 'cros', hence their name. One group actually took Bergerac. But the Governor of Aquitaine, the duc d'Epernon (the bellicose Protestant friend of Henry IV who refused to turn Catholic when the King did) sent troops to capture Buffarot, who was broken on the wheel in the market square of Monpazier.

The square is beautiful, with delightful arcades running around it, and a covered market hall with its old measures for grain. Markets are still held and there is a fair on the third Thursday of each month. In side streets are beautiful old houses, and the local inn, the 'France', is in a 13th-century house. It is kept very much in the style of old Périgord and serves meals from a cheap menu to a gastronomic Périgourdine feast.

Monpazier church is fortified, its nave is original from the 13th century, surrounds are from the 15th century, and the rose window is from 1550.

The formidable bulk of **Biron** castle stands on a high rock 8km south-west of Monpazier, and its mass of towers and walls show why it survived so many wars and revolutions. The Gontaut family owned it through 14 generations until the State took it over this century. It was taken and retaken, partly dismantled, repaired, altered and enlarged through almost every generation, so that it now looks from some angles like a disorderly group of fortresses with some almost standing on top of others. But it is impressive and its village is charming.

Started in the 12th century by the Gontaut family, it was occupied by the strange 'heretical' Albigensian sect until the infamous Simon de Montfort drove them out in his vicious and brutal 'crusade'. (He was the father of the Simon de Montfort, Earl of Leicester, who led the revolt of the English barons against Henry III of England.) The Albigensians were Christians who strove for perfection in this life, not in some remote heaven. They took their inspiration from mystics in the Middle East, stemming from 3rd-century Persia. They disagreed with much Catholic teaching; after St. Bernard had failed to convert them, Pope Innocent III decided in 1208 that they must be destroyed. He chose Montfort as his instrument of revenge and Montfort set about destroying, torturing and killing with fanatical zeal. Blessedly at the Siege of Toulouse, a stonemason threw a huge boulder at him and smashed his helmet and skull.

Louis VIII gave the castle back to the Gontauts, who played the English and French against each other. The Plantagenets took it for the English. The Earl of Derby took it in the Hundred Years' War. The family were always given it

Monpazier, fortified village built by the English, is the most attractive and best-preserved of these bastides.

back. Biron was raised to a Duchy in 1598 by Henry IV to reward Armand de Gontaut-Biron, the best of the bunch. A fine soldier, he fought for Henry III against Henry IV when he was the Protestant Henry of Navarre, but was chosen by Catherine de Médicis to negotiate peace terms. He then fought with Henry against the extremist Catholic Leaguers when Henry was King, and became a Marshal of France. He perished at the Siege of Epernay.

His son Charles was also a friend of Henry IV, who made him Marshal of France and Governor of Burgundy. He repaid the kindness by plotting against Henry with the King of Spain to dismember France. He was found out, but Henry forgave him. Then he did it again, and this time he was beheaded in the Bastille for treason. The family did not get the title of Lords of Biron back until 1723.

The village of Biron is within the outer walls. The building is too vast and of too many centuries to describe in detail, but you can see it any day, except on Tuesdays in mid-winter. The Renaissance additions add charm to the old sinister fortress, especially the courtyard, with a delightful Renaissance gallery and a lovely semi-circle entrance. The gem is the 16th-century Renaissance-style chapel with two storeys. The upper storey was for the Gontaut-Biron family and has two of their tombs. The lower chapel was for servants and villagers, who entered from the village. Inside it is worth seeing the state hall, the fine monumental staircase and the vast kitchen paved with huge stone slabs.

Sarlat, Beynac, Domme

Sarlat's captivating charm and atmosphere of contentment survives even the hordes of visitors and cars which invade it in mid-summer. It is described in official French guides as the most attractive medieval town in France to have preserved intact its ancient buildings. But it is far more than that. Side by side with its medieval masterpieces are superb Renaissance mansions, and it is impossible to wander through its little streets and alleyways without spotting some new treasure which you missed last time, be it a whole house or just a door or even a door-knocker.

Travel writers and tour operators are often accused of over-publicising beauty spots or delightful country hotels and 'spoiling' them, but it was the French Government which deliberately restored old Sarlat and publicised it as a tourist attraction back in 1964 — and for good reason. Agriculture had been declining in this whole area of France since the turn of the century. The French law of inheritance, dividing farms between all the children, had broken them down into such small units that few could make a living from the land. Wartime neglect meant that few

Hôtel de Maleville in Sarlat, originally three houses, was knocked into one in the 16th century

farmers had modern machinery or the means of buying it. Market towns like Sarlat were declining with the farms. The young were leaving the land for cities to take part in the post-war industrial boom and the new 'technological France'. Farm cottages were being abandoned. The French Government could see little future for small farm units in a world of sophisticated farm machinery. So they encouraged tourism and holiday homes. A Frenchman who bought a cottage to modernise as a second home was given seductive subsidies and easy loans. Sarlat, with its ancient houses, set in some of the most pleasant scenery in France and in the heart of the old Dordogne châteaux country, was a natural centre for tourism and leisure. A plan was drawn up to restore and safeguard the buildings and old streets of Sarlat; happily, the restoration was carried out with flair and sympathy.

For the saving of Sarlat we must thank Général de Gaulle's Minister of Cultural Affairs, André Malraux, art historian, novelist, Resistance leader and flamboyant character who lived in the Dordogne, fought in it, and who mentioned Sarlat specifically when he introduced a plan in 1962 for the protection and restoration of buildings or sections of towns of historic or architectural importance (see box).

The one atrocity committed against old Sarlat was in 1837 when, in the name of progress and to the joy of the local dignitaries, a road was cut right through the middle of the old quarter,

André Malraux

André Malraux, and his friend Josette Clotis, moved to Sarlat just before the Second World War. The old houses and streets captured the heart of this art historian and imaginative novelist. But when war came he joined the French army and was captured and imprisoned by the Germans. He escaped and hid in the village of Roquebrune on the Mediterranean, still unoccupied by the Germans. But he went back to the Dordogne in 1942 to join the Resistance. He contacted de Gaulle in London and other Resistance fighters in France and became 'Colonel Berger', commanding the FFI Resistance group covering Dordogne, Lot and Corrèze.

He was wounded, captured, and imprisoned in Toulouse. When the Germans fled Toulouse to avoid the advancing Allies, he took over the prison. He was a flamboyant character and de Gaulle shrewdly made him Minister of Propaganda. In 1958 he was made Minister of Cultural Affairs and in 1962 introduced a law for the protection and restoration of buildings and whole sectors of towns; and before he left the ministry in 1968, he made sure that the work was well under way under the direction of the Société d'Economie Mixte (SEMIRESA). Sarlat had been mentioned specifically in the bill. And no place in France has been restored with more care and sympathy. Malraux, who died in 1975 at the age of 74, deserves the plaque in his honour on the wall of a group of beautifully restored old buildings in the town.

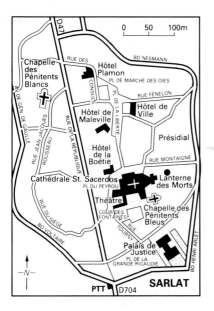

slicing through streets and destroying old houses. Officially called rue de la République, it has always been known locally as the 'Traverse'.

Sarlat has to be explored on foot. In high tourist season, cars are banned from some parts of town — and at any time driving under arches and through the narrow streets, which are so much worth exploring, would be a nightmare.

There is a fine view of the town at the southern end from the public gardens above the Law Courts (Palais de Justice). These gardens were laid out in the 17th century to the plan of Le Nôtre, Louis XIV's gardener from Versailles, at the request of Bishop François de Salignac, uncle of the great Fénelon. Originally the Bishop's private gardens, they are still extremely attractive.

To enjoy Sarlat to the full, you must take alleys and turnings at a whim and see what you discover. But do get a town map or you might miss some of

the more obvious treasures while discovering smaller and more secretive ones. In place de la Grande-Rigaudie, below the Law Courts, is a crumbling statue of Etienne de la Boétie, faithful friend of Montaigne (see box). The Renaissance house with pointed gable and mullioned windows where he was born is on the north-east corner of place du Peyrou (see below). North from Grande-Rigaudie is Cour des Fontaines, with an ancient fountain that still works. This was the site in the 6th century of a Benedictine monastery which had grown by the 12th century into a powerful abbey controlling 85 churches from here to Toulouse. The monks ruled both religious and temporal life of Sarlat until the merchants rebelled at the end of the 13th century and won the freedom to elect their own consul and representatives. The Pope, who came from Cahors, consoled the monks by making Sarlat into a Bishopric, and it had bishops until the Revolution. The original abbey was by the river Cruse, which now flows underground in Sarlat.

Then comes the 12th-century Chapelle des Pénitents Bleus, the chapel of the Upper Class citizens. The poorer folk had their chapel, Chapelle des Pénitents Blancs, across the Traverse, rather fittingly in rue Jean-Jacques Rousseau, which has several convents and walled gardens.

Between the Blue Penitents' chapel and the Cathedral is the ancient abbey cemetery made into a pleasant terraced garden which still has some of the 12th–15th-century tombstones. Up steps at the end is the old Lanterne des Morts, a 12th-century tower with a high conical stone roof. No one is quite sure what the tower was for, although there are some firm theories. The most

The Saturday market in Sarlat spreads over many streets and squares. This is in place de la Liberté

favoured is that it was erected in the last part of the 12th century to commemorate a miracle by St. Bernard. He was the man who tried to convert the Albigenois sect by persuasion before the Pope lost patience and had them slaughtered by Simon de Montfort. When Bernard preached in Sarlat, he blessed bread and told people that if they ate it when they were sick they would recover. It

seems that they did, and St. Bernard's tower was built in thanks. It was called the Lantern to the Dead later. It could have been a funeral chapel, a place where bodies were kept awaiting burial, or a place where bodies were put to await burning during the Plague.

The present cathedral was built in the 16th and 17th centuries, but the Romanesque belfry is obviously from

76

carried in procession around the town twice a year by the Catholics. The cathedral had to be reconsecrated in 1273 when a monk shot and killed his abbot in the choir with a bow and arrow.

It is a pleasant enough building but not so exciting as the old bishop's palace on the south side, now a theatre. This was built by the Italian Cardinal Gaddi when he was made Bishop of Sarlat in 1533. He brought with him from the Médicis court in Florence workmen and artists to build and decorate his palace, and the Italian influence is plain, particularly in ornament details and the polygon tower. The building has two storeys in stone, topped by one in brick.

On the opposite corner of place du Peyrou is Hôtel de la Boétie, where Montaigne's friend Etienne de la Boétie was born in 1530. It has been beautifully restored. These 'hôtels', of course, were private mansions, not hotels as we know them. There are more beautifully restored medieval and Renaissance buildings with balconies through a passageway by the Boétie house, with a plaque to André Malraux.

The Sarlat tourist office is in another fine 16th-century dwelling, Hôtel de Maleville, in place de la Liberté. One façade is French Renaissance, another Italian Renaissance. It was created in the 16th century, by joining three houses together, by Jean Vienne, a local man who rose to high office under Henry IV partly because Henry's mistress Gabrielle d'Estrées took a liking to him. Henry and Gabrielle's medallions are on either side of the front door. Eastward is the old Présidial, the Royal law courts until the Revolution. Place de la Liberté runs north into the market place where during the last

an earlier church, though its bulbous top was added in the 18th century. The original 12th-century church was dedicated to St. Sacerdos, who was supposed to have cured people of leprosy. His body was buried in the church, but during the Wars of Religion the Protestant de Vivans had it cremated and the ashes thrown away. A few bones survived, and they are

77

Etienne de la Boétie

Outside Sarlat, where he rates as the most famous son, Etienne de la Boétie is now remembered mostly as the faithful friend of the writer Montaigne. But his talent was equal to Montaigne's in some ways, although he died at 36.

Boétie was born in 1530 in the beautiful house his father built by Sarlat Cathedral. At 24 he had already become a counsellor in the Bordeaux Parlement, where a few years later he met Montaigne. Undoubtedly he influenced Montaigne's thoughts and writings enormously, for they were very close friends, and Boétie became known to many people after his early death through Montaigne's essay on Friendship. But Boétie had been writing without publishing. He had translated classics from the Greek. He had written sonnets for a mistress he called 'Dourdouigne' (Dordogne). And he had written powerful essays, too, including one called 'Voluntary Servitude'. This was included among the works Montaigne had published after Boétie's death. Subversive stuff for those days, it submitted that the root of a tyrant's power was not his own strength or ability but the sycophancy of those who supported him to gain position or profit. He found it unbelievable that people could prefer position and profit to personal freedom. Those who accepted tyranny, who did not rebel against it, were as guilty as the tyrants.

This essay made little impression on the French until the rise of the great Radicals and the early Socialists in the last century. But then, let us face it, the French have always tolerated and even admired 'strong men' and tyrants such as Louis XIII, Louis XIV, their Revolutionary leaders and above all Napoléon, more readily than these have been accepted among Scandinavians or Anglo-Saxons.

We confess that it took the rise of a tyrant — Hitler — to bring our attention to Boétie's writing. And we have still seen only extracts from his writings, not the full text. A modern translation could help to widen the understanding of his philosophy.

weeks of July and first of August classical drama is played by groups of visiting actors, including some from the Comédie Française. There are many more fine old houses in the streets and squares around here.

Through the market you reach place du Marché des Oies, the old goose market, where these days the goose you buy is as likely to be a tin of confit as a live goose in a cage. There are good markets in Sarlat on Wednesdays and Saturdays. The Saturday market is also in place de la Grande-Rigaudie, which has a useful car park the rest of the week. Around the corner from place du Marché des Oies, in rue des Consuls, is Hôtel Plamon, an impressive beautiful house built in the 14th century for the Selves de Plamon family of cloth merchants. The ground floor is like a courtyard with arcades, and may have been used for selling cloth, or more likely for dyeing it. Living quarters start on the first floor, reached by a monumental staircase. Here are beautifully restored Gothic windows. Follow the rue des Consuls across the Traverse and you are in a little maze of small medieval streets and narrow twisting, sloping alleys. We can remember when the houses here were even more tightly packed and some almost derelict. Some demolition was done during renovation. During this work 350 coins were found bearing the effigy of England's Black Prince. Sarlat was an English garrison town for ten years from 1360.

Though it retains so many old buildings and streets and lures so many tourists in mid-summer, Sarlat is very much a living, working commercial town, with good shops, hotels and restaurants. The old Madeleine Hôtel was a temple of superb Périgourdine dishes when Ogée Delbos kept it. Then the St. Albert became the place to taste these superb regional specialties. It still is. It tends to get crowded and noisy, especially in mid-summer or on weekends, and the service is friendly rather than quick and polished. But it is great fun and good value, though no place for a quiet tête-à-tête.

Nine kilometres north-west of Sarlat, off D47, is the castle of **Puymartin**, headquarters of local Catholics when the Protestants held Sarlat. It is beautiful — a 15th–16th-century building in golden stone, roofed with stone slates. Though it still has it battlemented walls and defence turrets, it looks truly peaceful in its field setting and is more attractive and interesting than many better-known châteaux. It is open from 1st April–15th September, on guided tours. Some of the decorations and furnishings are quite delightful. There are six fine Flemish tapestries

of scenes from the Trojan Wars, 18th-century Aubusson tapestries in a pleasant shade of green, and 18th-century wall paintings with mythological themes.

The stretch of the Dordogne river a few kilometres south of Sarlat, from St. Cyprien to Souillac, is one of the most attractive river stretches in France and extremely interesting, for it is so rich in historic castles and bastides with fascinating tales to tell.

St. Cyprien, which is joined by pretty roads to Le Bugue and Les Eyzies, does not quite reach the river. It is clamped in terraces to the side of a hill in a typical Dordogne setting of hills and woods, with old houses nestling around its massive church, part of a 12th-century Augustinian abbey, with a formidable square belfry keep. The

Many lovely old buildings in Sarlat have been faithfully restored.

79

Beynac castle — once a superb site for defence, now a superb site for views over the Dordogne

Castelnaud, an English stronghold, scowled across the Dordogne at Beynac, held by the French

81

inside, with ogival vaulting, looks like an enormous cathedral. St. Cyprien has a market on Sundays, which is useful.

The river winds delightfully eastward to Beynac-et-Cazenac on its northern bank, and here is one of the great historic castles of France. **Beynac** was one of the four baronies of Périgord, and the Lords of Beynac owned this castle, which played a major part in the Hundred Years' War. The other baronies were Biron, Bourdeilles and Mareuil.

The castle rises from the top of a great rock overlooking the river. It was a wonderful site for defence. Now it is a magnificent site for views. You can see right along the snaking river, which winds between hills topped with castles — Marqueyssac, Castelnaud, Fayrac, La Malartrie. Below, the village spreads in a narrow ribbon along the river bank.

Richard Coeur de Lion took Beynac castle in the 12th century. Instead of dismantling it, which was usual in those days, he put in Mercadier, a thug who pillaged the countryside.

On his crusade to wipe out the Albigensian religious sect, Simon de Montfort decided in 1214 that the owner of Beynac sympathised with the Albigensians, seized the castle and dismantled it. The Lord of Beynac had it rebuilt, which was a good thing for the French in the Hundred Years' War. The Dordogne marked the frontier between the French and the English, with the French occupying Beynac on the north bank, the English the mighty castle of Castelnaud across the river. They would scowl across the river at each other, keeping constant guard, and sometimes sending out raiding parties. It must have been hell to live in the nearby villages, which were pillaged and looted regularly.

The castle has a sheer drop of 150m on three sides, and the other was protected from attack by a double perimeter wall. The inner wall encloses a powerful quadrangular keep. In the living quarters inside are some lovely rooms, especially the barrel-vaulted great Hall of State where the nobles of Périgord used to meet. The adjoining oratory is decorated with Gothic frescoes from the 15th century, showing the Last Supper, a Christ at the foot of his cross, and members of the Beynac family. There is a fine Florentine staircase from the 17th century.

There has been some criticism of the restoration as being 'rebuilding'. However, nothing has been altered, but crumbling stone has been replaced with stone quarried from the same places that were used in the 14th century. Restoration has not quite finished.

In the village by the river is one of our favourite little old-style French family-run inns, the Bonnet Hôtel, still run by the Bonnet family, with the same family cooking and welcome. The terrace still has the same river view, and if you walk down the river towpath you are often alone. All that has changed is the hotel plumbing, which has improved, and the passing traffic.

Over the river bridge just downstream are the remains of **Castelnaud**, recently restored and open daily. Like Beynac, it was built in the 12th century to command the valleys of the Dordogne and Céou and has a wonderful panorama from its terrace. You can see across fields to a big loop in the Dordogne river and beyond to Beynac and la Roque-Gageac below a cliff. The Cazenac family owned the castle originally, but the dreaded Simon de Montfort grabbed it in 1214 during his

Josephine Baker

Josephine Baker, brought up in a cellar in the slums of St. Louis, joined an all-black dancing troupe at 19 for a tour of Europe. A year later she was top-billed artiste in Paris cabaret and was said to be the highest paid entertainer in Europe. The Folies Bergères billed her as 'The Charleston Queen'.

On a tour of the Dordogne in a Bugatti Royale in the 1930s she visited the Château of Les Milandes and fell in love with it. When the Second World War started in 1939, instead of fleeing to the US, which was not to come into the war for nearly two years, she returned to Les Milandes. And as the war went the Nazi way, she became more deeply involved, first risking her life hiding escaping RAF aircrew, Poles, and others, then working with the Resistance, for which she was given the Legion of Honour and rosette by de Gaulle.

After the War, she bought Les Milandes, married her agent Joe Bouillon and they both worked hard in show-business to pay for the renovation and improvement of the château, including restoring the 49-hectare park. They even opened a restaurant there.

Then she started to make a dream come true. She adopted children of different colours, races and religions to further the unity of the human race. They came from around the globe — French children and Finns, Koreans, South Americans, Africans from Algeria and the Ivory Coast. She housed and gave jobs to 70 local people.

All this was way beyond her means. She even opened a gambling casino in the grounds to help pay the expenses. Joe Bouillon was driven to despair by her spending — on others. They separated. In 1964 the château was sold.

We were taken to visit her by a group of French people not long before her dream collapsed. The children eating in a vast kitchen were well dressed, well fed, well supervised and happy. Josephine opened champagne for her guests, turned on the gramophone and danced. It was mid-afternoon. No one could have guessed that the château was near to bankruptcy.

anti-Albigensian campaign on the excuse that the owners were heretics. He must have liked Castelnaud, for instead of knocking it down, as was his wont, he restored it. But the owners took it back next year.

The English held it for much of the Hundred Years' War under the command for 25 years of a distinguished soldier Raymond de Sort. Then in the Wars of Religion came a

melodrama worthy of the most imaginative writer of historical romance. Alexandre Dumas would not have dared to use such an unlikely plot.

The younger son of Castelnaud's owner, Geoffroy de Caumont, was Abbot of Clairac in Agenais but had secretly become a Protestant. When his father and elder brother died, he inherited Castelnaud, left the church, and married Marguerite de Lustrac, who

Château de Fayrac, a magnificent 15th-century manor house facing Beynac across the Dordogne

was usually called Mme la Maréchale because she had previously been married to the Maréchal de St. André. Geoffroy died in 1572 of poisoning after eating mushrooms. Three months later his wife gave birth to a daughter Anne, who was a very rich heiress indeed. Henry III made her uncle, Jean de Cars, her guardian and he determined to get the money by marrying her to his son Prince de Carency. But the Seigneur of Biron was after her and

the money for his son, too. So Jean de Cars kidnapped the child, who was only seven years old, and forcibly married her to the Prince. Five years later her 18-year-old husband was killed in a duel by the 18-year-old Charles de Biron. Anne was 12 and a widow. Jean de Cars then tried to marry her to his second son. Mme la Maréchale would have nothing to do with it, and she was backed by the Duke of Mayenne, who also fancied the girl and

Views over the Dordogne from Domme surpass even those from Beynac and Roque-Gageac

her fortune for his son. She was kidnapped again and married to Mayenne's son in Paris. He was only nine! Henry III tired of the arguments and sent the girl to be looked after by the deeply Catholic Duchess of Nemours, who converted her to Catholicism. At 18 she was kidnapped and married for the third time, to François d'Orléans, Comte de St. Pol. They had a son, but St. Pol was such a wastrel that she left him, taking her son with her. The

son, a page to Louis XIII, was killed at the Siege of Montpelier. His mother had had enough. She retired to a convent, whereupon Mme la Maréchale disinherited her and gave Castelnaud to her cousin, Jacques de Caumont, to keep it in the family. It now contains a museum of siege instruments, arms, etc.

This is a superb area for seeing castles of many sizes and shades of importance. **Château de Fayrac**, just downstream, facing Beynac, was under the control of the Lords of Castelnaud. It stands on the river banks and looks quite different from different angles. It is still quite magnificent. The north side, facing Beynac, looks fearsome, with two massive round towers with pepperpot roofs. The south side, though approached by a drawbridge and gate set in crenellated walls, looks more like a manor house when viewed from the courtyard, has smaller round and square towers and a terrace overlooking the Dordogne river. Built between the 14th and 17th centuries, it was unusually well restored last century.

Continue past Fayrac on the little riverside road westward and you reach a village called Les Milandes. Here in 1478 the Lord of Castelnaud, François de Caumont, built as a wedding present for his wife a lovely Renaissance château, with terraces and gardens to the river. The Caumonts lived there until the revolution, which it happily survived. It was extended in the 19th century. It was run-down in the 1930s when it was discovered by 'La Perle Noire' of Paris cabaret, Josephine Baker, the slum-child from St. Louis, Missouri, who by the age of 20 was Queen of the Folies Bergères. From Les Milandes she ran an arm of the French Resistance and here she hid British RAF pilots, Poles, Belgians, escaping from the Nazis. And it was here after the War when she bought the château that she set up her dream 'World Village', giving a home to orphaned children of different races, religions and nationalities. Alas, the dream ended in 1964 when she had to sell the château because of a mountain of debts (see box). Some of her furniture and effects are still in the château, mixed with possessions of the Caumont family. It is open daily from

mid March–mid November. The garden and park are still beautiful.

The D703 pretty but crowded road from Beynac along the north side of the river passes the ruins of the Château of Marqueyssac to **La Roque-Gageac**, a quite remarkable village. It clings so precariously to a cliff above the Dordogne that you expect some of the houses to fall in the river. In fact, rocks have tumbled down on occasion, killing people and destroying houses. The worst was in the winter of 1956–1957, when a number of houses with people inside did actually fall into the river.

It is a beautiful village. Its winding alleys and streets are lined with the ochre houses of craftsmen and peasants and the mansions of the merchants, climbing up the tall grey cliff-face to the holm-oaks, the scene often reflected in the water below. A

The restored village of Roque-Gageac is huddled beneath a steep cliff beside the Dordogne river.

lovely view is from the square in front of the 12th-century church above the village. The village had great strategic importance in the Hundred Years' War, when the English failed to take it, and in the days of *gabare* traffic on the river when wine was taken down to be exported. **Château de la Malartrie**, the seemingly-15th-century house at the west end of the village, is a 19th-century fake — 'replica' is the kinder word. **Manoir de Tarde**, at the foot of the rocks, is a genuine 16th-century manor house flanked by a turret with pepper-pot roof. It was the home of the Tarde family. Much of the knowledge we have of this area around Sarlat comes from the chronicles of Jean Tarde, who was born here. He was a distinguished humanist, mathematician and astronomer, who knew Galileo. Gabriel de la Tarde, who lived here in the 19th century, was a renowned sociologist.

D703 continues to be a most attractive road as it winds eastward near or alongside the river through Vitrac where you can fish and swim to Château de Montfort. But first you must cross the river 3km after La Roque-Gageac to see **Domme** — with Monpazier the most beautiful of the bastides and far more spectacular.

Built in 1280 for Philip the Bold, whose boldness was often mere braggadocio, it has a panoramic view from its belvedere (the Barre) which surpasses even the views from Beynac and La Roque-Gageac, both of which you can see. It is built on a rocky crag overlooking the countryside of the Dordogne valley, and you have a superb view of the poplar-lined river snaking through fields with a far backcloth of hills. But the town itself, in golden stone, is more beautiful. A wriggling road reaches a narrow gateway which takes you into the outer square. This is the Porte des Bos, one of three gates piercing Domme's great walls. A rampart walk reaches the arched Porte de la Combe, and farther around the walls a tiny road from the river reaches the Porte des Tours, flanked by two massive semi-circular towers. In one of these are names and arms of Knights Templars imprisoned here in the 14th century, when Philip le Bel arrested almost all of them in one single coup, accused them of appalling crimes, to which many confessed under torture, killed most of them and had the Order banned by the Pope.

Domme is an orderly town, despite some of its roads being narrow, and is made more beautiful by the proud local people who grow flowers and vines up their balconies and outside staircases.

Below the covered market near the church is the entrance to caves used as hiding places by the villagers in the Hundred Years' War and in the Wars of Religion. A series of small chambers about 450m long has been cleared for visits (1st April–31 October) and some have slender white stalactites, as well as pillars formed by stalactites and stalagmites meeting. Bones of bison and rhinoceros found in the caves are on show.

A cliff walk (Promenade des Falaises) alongside the public gardens leads to a viewing table from which the panorama is even wider than from the belvedere.

We have eaten for many years on the terrace of the Esplanade Hôtel at Domme, overlooking the river valley and thought the food and view superb. These days it has a Michelin star but compared with many starred restaurants is not outrageously expensive.

The 13th-century buildings of Domme are delightful

The spectacular site of Montfort castle made it so important that it was destroyed and rebuilt four times

Though Château Malartrie at Roque Gageac looks pure 15th-century, it was built in the 19th.

Philip the Bold believed Domme to be impregnable, and it was, until the Wars of Religion when the great Protestant leader Geoffroy de Vivans, who was born at Fayrac castle and knew the area well, proved that even in those warlike days brains could baffle brawn. He took Domme without disturbing a stone. With 30 men, he climbed the cliff-face of the Barre in the night, a trick regarded as so impossible that there were no guards on that side. Inside the sleeping town, he and his men beat drums and blew trumpets loudly to cause pandemonium, and before the guards or people could get organised they had opened the tower gate and let in his army. French guide writers get quite indignant about the way he took castles 'by trickery', but it would seem better than knocking half the castles down and killing a great many people,

like others did — particularly the Leaguers. But he did spoil it this time by burning down half the church, then knocking down most of the 11th-century Cénac Priory nearby.

Once Henry was crowned Henry IV, called himself a Catholic and Protestantism was no longer illegal after the Nantes Declaration, everyone except a few fanatics, mostly Leaguers, tired of the war and Vivans sold Domme to the Catholics for 40,000 livres.

Back across the river past Vitrac, the Dordogne makes a big horseshoe loop, almost meeting itself. This is the Cingle de Montfort, the Montfort Meander, as the French translate it. **Montfort** castle is perched picturesquely high on a rock falling sheer to the Dordogne river. It is a hotch-potch of styles from several centuries but looks charming. Alas, it is understandably not open to the public.

The destructive Simon de Montfort gave it its name by destroying it completely in 1214 after taking it from Bernard de Casnac. Simon's lust for destruction in the name of the Pope was quite extraordinary even by the standards of those days. It was rebuilt, taken over by the Turenne family and captured by the English in the Hundred Years' War after sieges. Pons de Turenne got it back, but in the Wars of Religion the Turenne family became Protestants and made Montfort a Huguenot stronghold. The result of all these battles was that Montfort was badly damaged and rebuilt three times, which is why it has many styles of building, from medieval through Renaissance and Classical to some 19th-century restoration.

Beautiful Domme village was a formidable fortress when built in 1282.

Roads on both sides of the river are well worth exploring for some way after Cingle de Montfort, but it is better to cross to the smaller D50 on the south bank to reach **Château de Fénelon**. This is where the great Fénelon, writer, priest and finally Archbishop of Cambrai was born in 1651 — François de Salignac de la Mothe-Fénelon. He was one of eleven children. Alas, you may not see inside the castle. Visits are confined to the chapel and a room showing items related to Fénelon. There is also a nice little collection of vintage cars. Built from the 13th to 15th centuries, Fénelon castle was built very much for war, with three lines of defence, fortified doorways, and outer walls flanked by defence towers to prevent an attack from the terrace on which it stands. But the northern entrance façade was softened in the 16th century and has a pleasant horseshoe staircase to the courtyard. The château was very correctly restored in the 1930s by the Maleville family.

The D50 road from Fénelon to Souillac beside the Dordogne is outstandingly pleasant.

91

Hotels and Restaurants

A = very expensive, B = expensive, C = moderately expensive, D = moderate, E = inexpensive.

BADEFOLS-SUR-DORDOGNE — 24150 Lalinde. Lou Cantou on D29 (53.22.50. 26). Good meals, fair prices. Open 1st Apr–30th Sept. Meals D–E; rooms D–E.

BERGERAC — 24100 Dordogne. Le Cyrano, 2 bd Montaigne (53.57.02.76). Typical provincial hotel with enclosed pavement terrace. Good cuisine, both regional and lighter modern, excellent value. Meals D–E; rooms E.

BEYNAC — 24220 St. Cyprien. Bonnet on D703 (53.29.50.01). Delightful old hotel. Run by Bonnet family for generations. True Périgordian dishes. Plumbing has been improved. Meals C–E; rooms E. Closed mid Oct–mid April.

LE BUGUE — 24260 Dordogne. Royal Vézère Hôtel (Restaurant l'Albuca), pl Hôtel-de-Ville (53.07.20.01). Fine views of Vézère river and countryside from roof terrace. Open end April–1st Oct. Meals B–D; rooms C–D.
Auberge du Noyer at Le Reclaud de Bouny-Bas (5-km west from Le Bugue along D703) (53.07.11.73). Lovely 18th-century farmhouse renovated by English couple. Well-furnished; quiet garden; pool. Meals D–E; rooms D–E. Shut Nov–15th Mar.

DOMME — 24250 Dordogne. Esplanade, promenade de la Barre (53.28.31.41) (see p. 87). Superb views over Dordogne (150m below) to Sarlat. Superb classical cooking by René Gillard. Meals B–E; rooms D–E.

LES EYZIES — 24620 Dordogne. Centenaire (53.06.97.18). Roland Mazère is one of the best chefs in France. He is reviving Périgourdine cooking while inventing modern dishes. One of the best wine lists in France, too. Pool. 'Body building' gymnasium. Modern bedrooms. Open 1st Apr–early Nov. Meals A–C; rooms B–E.
Cro-Magnon route de Périgueux (53.06.97.06). Nice garden; very good cooking. True regional dishes. Open end Apr–mid Oct. Meals A–E; rooms D–E.
Centre, pl Mairie (53.06.97.13). Attractive old house in shady square with pretty garden by river Vézère. Pure Périgourdine cooking, remarkable value. Open 15th Mar–mid Nov. Meals B–E; rooms D.

LALINDE — 24150 Dordogne. Château Hôtel, rue Verdun (53.61.01.82). Formidable little 13th-century fortress with pointed towers turned into comfortable hotel with terrace overhanging Dordogne river. Entirely renovated in 1993. Open 1st Mar–15th Nov. Meals C–E; rooms D–E.

LIMEUIL – 24510 Ste. Alvère. Beauregard Hôtel (Restaurant les Terrasses), route de Trémolat (53.22.03.15). Country hotel above Dordogne river. Magnificent position. Good cooking. Meals C–E; rooms D–E. Closed 1 Oct–1 May.

MONBAZILLAC — 24240 Sigoulés. Relais de la Diligence, route Eymet D933

(53.58.30.48). Modernised old inn with fine vineyard views from terrace. Good value. Meals C–E; rooms E.

Closerie St. Jacques, Le Bourg (53.58.37.77). Restaurant in large old house; very comfortable. Very good cooking; less expensive menu good value. Meals B–C.

MONPAZIER — 24540 Dordogne. France, rue St. Jacques (53.61.60.06). Little old country inn in 13th-century house, deliberately left unchanged. Nice atmosphere. Cheap menu excellent value; gastronomic Périgourdine menu, too. Meals C–E; rooms D–E.

MAUZAC — 24150 Lalinde. La Métairie (at Milac, 2.5-km north) (53.22.50.47). Converted old stone farmhouse; pretty garden, pool. Attractive bedrooms. Meals B–E; rooms A–B. Closed mid Oct–1 April.

LA ROQUE-GAGEAC — 24250 Domme. Belle Etoile on D703 (53.29.51.44). Old house attractive rooms overlooking river. Open end Mar–mid Oct. Meals C–E; rooms D–E.

ST. JULIEN DE CREMPSE — 24140 Villamblard. Manoir de Grand Vignoble (12-km north of Bergerac by N21, D107) (53.24.23.18). Beautiful Louis XIV manor in park; pool, stables (60 horses), deer, yak, camels. Regional and modern cooking. Meals C–D; rooms C–D.

SARLAT — 24200 Dordogne. St. Albert, pl Pasteur (53.59.01.09). Old-style hotel with modernised bedrooms; old-style Périgourdine meals. Busy, popular. Meals C–E; rooms D–E.
Hostellerie Marcel, 8 av de Selves (53.59.21.98). Superb value menus. Meals D–E; rooms E. Open 1st Mar–15th Nov.
Rossignol, 15 rue Fénelon (53.31.02.30). Good regional and bourgeoise cuisine. Excellent value. Meals C–E.
La Hoirie (2-km south by D704) (53.59.05.62). Open mid Mar–mid Nov. Charming old hunting lodge in gardens. Quiet. Meals B–D; rooms C–D.
La Ferme (at Caudon-de-Vitrac, 12-km south-east by D46, D703) (53.28.33.35). Enormous meals of local country dishes at bargain prices. Charming old farmhouse. We were first customers many years ago. Still in same family. Meals D–E.

SAUSSIGNAC — 24240 Sigoulés. Hôtel à Saussignac (53.27.92.08). Modern hotel in wine village centre. Meals D–E; rooms E.

TRÉMOLAT — 24510 Ste. Alvère. Vieux Logis (53.22.80.06). Delightful old Logis in lovely gardens; superb antique furniture; irreproachable service; fine cooking. Booking essential. Henry Miller came for two days, stayed a month. Meals B–D; rooms A–B.
Panoramic (2.5km along Cingle de Trémolat by D31) (53.22.80.42). Superb views from terrace. Good value meals. Meals D–E; rooms D–E.

VILLEFRANCHE-DU-PÉRIGORD — 24550 Dordogne. Commerce, pl de la Liberté (53.29.90.11). Closed 30 Nov–15 March. Charming stone building with arcade making terrace. Good views, family atmosphere. Meals B–E; rooms D–E.

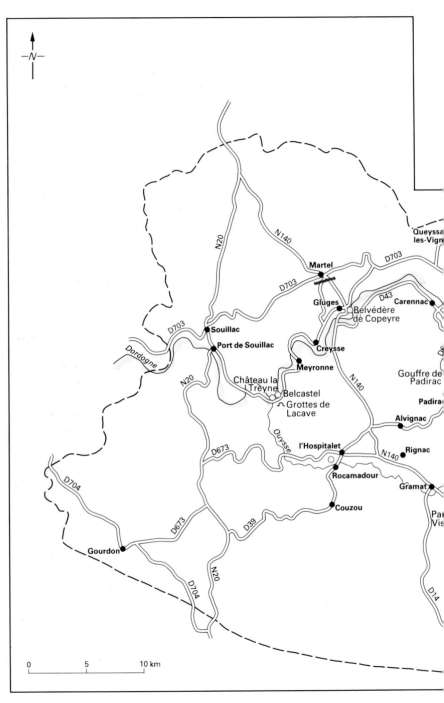

6
Souillac, Rocamadour to St. Céré

The river Dordogne winds and snakes so elusively eastwards from **Souillac** into Lot that to follow it you must take a series of tiny roads, and even then you will lose it for stretches. But it is well worth map-reading your way along it, for the roads pass through delightful country and hamlets and there are many treasures on the way. Be prepared to cross and recross the river to see the most of them.

Start from the right bank at **Port de Souillac** and switch to the left in time to see **Château la Treyne**. Perched on a clifftop falling vertically to the river, formidable but beautiful, it has the true elegance of a 17th century château with a tower and the belligerence of the original 14th century fortress. Tastefully furnished, it has become a Relais et Châteaux hotel in lovely parkland. The gardens can be visited (1st June–15th September except Mondays). Just upstream where the river Ouysse joins the Dordogne is **Belcastel**; and it really is aptly named 'bel', especially in sunlight when the river shines silver below the sheer white cliffs on which it stands. Part of the main wing and the chapel, which you can visit, are from the Middle Ages. The rest was reconstructed last century. But the joy of Belcastel is to go on the terrace, which is open, for the superb views of the meeting of the two rivers, and the green hills and valleys all around.

Just eastward where the Dordogne makes a deep cutting through the Gramat Causse is a series of caves at the foot of cliffs called **Grottes de Lacave**, discovered by a student in 1902. They are impressive and interesting but suffer in comparison to the great caves and underground river at Padirac farther east.

A small underground railway and a lift take you to an underground platform where you walk for about 1½km return journey. The shapes of some rocks look like animals, people and buildings. There are stalactites and stalagmites, underground rivers and pools, a remarkable fluorescent lake chamber and a beautiful Hall of Wonders. The caves are open from 1st April to mid-October. (1 hour tours.)

The road now follows the river through attractive rocks and cliffs to a suspension bridge over the Dordogne where there is a view of the village of **Meyronne**, built into the cliffs, and of the river itself. Cross the bridge and take the D114 along the willow-shaded river bank to the charming village of **Creysse**. Its delightful narrow streets of brown-roofed houses with front steps lead to a narrow alley. This climbs steeply to a very old church beside a pleasant terrace and the remains of a castle, perched on a rock. The little main square shaded by plane trees has a wonderful other-century atmosphere.

Gluges, the next village, is in a beautiful riverside setting at the bottom of cliffs. From nearby **Belvédère de Copeyre** beside D32 is a fine view of the river and, on the other side of the Dordogne, of the Cirque de Mont-

St. Céré is a charming market town and fine touring centre

From Belcastel's terraces you have wonderful views of the Dordogne.

valent — a road running beside the river and rising sometimes above it.

Before you cross to take the cirque and the D43 to Carennac, follow the D23 from just west of Gluges for 7km to **Martel**. History was made in this 'town of seven towers', and you can still see many excellent medieval buildings. It is a market centre for truffles and nuts.

In 732 the Moors were sweeping up Europe, threatening to turn what we now call France and probably lands far beyond into Moslem domains. Christianity itself was in danger, as well as the freedom of the people of Europe. Charles Martel stopped the Moorish armies at Poitiers, then chased them into Aquitaine. A few years later he struck them again, on this very spot, wiping them out. In thanks to God for victory over the Infidels, he built a church here. Soon a town grew up around it. The town was called Martel

and took as its crest three hammers, the favourite weapon of Charles Martel. Martel was elected King of the Franks. His grandson was the Emperor Charlemagne, King of the Franks, Roman Emperor, and the ruler who tried to bring order, Christianity and culture to Europe. Alas, his successors were weaklings, his Empire fell apart, and Europe is still seeking unity.

The town of Martel was the scene in the 12th century of an English Royal tragedy which was the beginning of the end of the Plantagenets. By marrying the vivacious, intelligent and wayward Eleanor of Aquitaine, whose marriage to the King of France had been annulled because she was accused of adultery on a Crusade, Henry Plantagenet added Aquitaine to his lands. He was already Duke of Normandy and Count of Anjou. Shortly after, he became King Henry II of England also. But Eleanor had a certain reputation with troubadours of her court, and the angry Henry locked her in a tower. He had been genuinely in love with her — unusual for medieval kings and queens. Their four sons sided with their mother, the eldest, Henry, openly and immediately. His father had honoured him by having him crowned associate king and his successor, and he was known as the Young King. The nobles had to swear allegiance to him. He was also known as Henry Courtmantel because he favoured the fashionable French short cloak. But he copied that idea from his father, who earlier had the same nickname. Two King Henrys, two Henry-short-mantles. Very confusing for their subjects!

When Eleanor was imprisoned Young Henry took up arms against his father and pillaged Turenne and Quercy. Henry II disinherited him, gave his lands to the third son, Richard Coeur de Lion, and stopped his allowance.

Henry Courtmantel was broke, surrounded and desperate. To pay his soldiers he plundered the treasure houses of abbeys, then committed the great sacrilege of looting from Rocamadour the shrine and precious stones of St. Amadour, as well as the sword of Roland which he sold. The story goes that as he left Rocamadour, the bell began to toll, and he took it as a sign of God's anger. He fled to Martel where he arrived in a fever. He confessed his sins. Henry II was sent for to forgive him. Henry was busy at the siege of Limoges and just sent a messenger, who found Henry Courtmantel lying on a bed of cinders with a cross at his breast. He died shortly after.

The house where he died — a mansion flanked with a round tower now called Maison Fabri — is in the

Martel's Hôtel Turenne and restaurant Quercy are in traditional Quercy golden stone.

interesting place des Consuls with several other fine buildings. One is Hôtel de la Raymondie, a superb house of the Turenne family, begun in 1280 and finished in 1330. Dominated by a crenellated belfry, it has a tower at each corner. Rose windows face into the courtyard. Now it is the town hall and tourist office.

The Gothic church here still shows signs of fortification, with two watch towers and a line of battlements. The belfry, 48m high, doubled as a defensive keep, with narrow loopholes for archers.

A Romanesque tympanum below the porch, showing Christ in glory surrounded by angels, is worth seeing, so are the 16th-century stained-glass windows in the chancel.

Relics of the perimeter walls show how heavily fortified Martel was in the Middle Ages, with towers and gateways still existing. There are some fine houses in the old town, too, particularly in rue Droite leading into place des Consuls and a small street by Hôtel de la Raymondie, rue Tournemire. The tourist office will tell you about tours of old Martel, visiting the seven towers and tasting *eau de noix*, the digestif made from walnuts which is a traditional speciality of Lot. So is *eau de prunes*, made among other places at Carennac, eastward on the left bank of the Dordogne. We have drunk this fairly powerful digestif often enough now to enjoy it.

Carennac is a lovely little place. Its houses with brown-tiled roofs cluster around the remains of a priory on the river banks. The writer–priest Fénelon lived here and many of the houses date from the 16th and 17th centuries. All that is left of Fenelon's priory–deanery is the priory tower, a fortified gateway and the prior's dwelling, called the château, where temporary exhibitions are held. The church of St. Pierre has a 12th-century doorway with a superb carved tympanum of the Toulouse school. Peaceful cloisters beyond have Romanesque and Flamboyant galleries.

With the isle of Calypso in the centre of the river, this is a most attractive place for swimming, canoeing, fishing and watersports.

The priory was founded in the 10th century and later attached to the great, powerful and rich Abbey of Cluny. When a student in Cahors, Fénelon spent his vacations in Carennac with his uncle, who was senior prior. In 1681 when his uncle died, Fénelon was made commendatory prior and, unlike most commendatory benificiaries, who just took the money and kept clear of the job, he stayed there for 15 years until made Archbishop of Cambrai. In Carennac he wrote 'Télémaque', the adventures of Ulysses' son, left unpublished until turned into a tract for the

Montal — a lovely, romantic Renaissance château, near St. Céré, which arose from ruins

Old houses in the delightful village of Carennac surround the beautiful priory where Fénelon once lived.

education of Louis XIV's son, the Duke of Burgundy, to whom Fénelon had been made tutor. Louis regarded it as a satire on his court and was very angry. The people of Carennac renamed Ile Barrae in the river Calypso's Isle in honour of his story.

Just after Carennac is the place where other waters meet the Dordogne. The Dordogne itself has come down from the north, through Beaulieu, the Cère comes in from the east, the Bave from the south.

An archbishop of Bourges named a beautiful place on the Dordogne river 'Beaulieu' around 850 and founded an abbey there with monks from Cluny. The monks built the 12th-century church in the Limousin–Romanesque style. The magnificent sculptured doorway, showing Greek influence, is regarded as one of the great masterpieces of Romanesque sculpture. It was carved by Toulouse craftsmen who were responsible for others at Moissac and Souillac. The superb tympanum shows the Last Judgement, with prophets on supporting pillars and scenes from the Temptation and Daniel and the Lion.

Take the attractive D41 from just south of Beaulieu to Queyssac-les-Vignes, a village set among vineyards and hills. From the top of a restored tower, reached through the courtyard of the village inn, there is a splendid panorama of the Dordogne Valley, with cirque de Montvalent, Carennac and Castelnau castle one way, St. Laurent-les-Tours at St. Céré to the south-east, and Turenne castle northwards.

The most formidable medieval castle in France, **Castelnau**, stands on a spur over the village of Prudhomat near to where the river Cère joins the Dordogne. It is a magnificent medieval pile with red stone ramparts, built in the 11th century and extended, in the Hundred Years' War, until it was 5km around with a garrison of 1,500 men and 100 horses. It was abandoned in the 18th century, suffered in the Revolution, and caught fire in 1851, but was carefully restored between 1896 and 1932. Goodness knows what it would have cost to restore today.

Some of the old ramparts have been replaced by an avenue of trees and, as you follow them, you have some fine views of the Cère and Dordogne valleys.

The plan of the castle is a triangle with round towers at each corner and projecting towers on the sides. Three perimeter walls still exist, and in the big main court is a tower 62m high. Inside the château are a lapidary museum, fine old Aubusson and Beauvais tapestries, with 15th-century stained-glass in the oratory.

The medieval barons of Castelnau called themselves the Second Barons of

Christendom, paying homage only to the Counts of Toulouse. They had vast power in Quercy and beyond. In 1184 Count Raymond of Toulouse gave the overlordship of Castelnau to the Viscount of Turenne. The Baron of Castelnau was so insulted that he switched his allegiance from Toulouse to Philip Augustus, King of France. War started between Turenne and Castelnau.

When Philip's son Louis VIII came to the throne, he decided in favour of Turenne, but the fief was only symbolic. The Baron of Castelnau had to pay each year to Turenne just one egg. So every year, with full pomp and ceremony, four oxen bore a new-laid egg to Turenne.

The nearby village of **Bretenoux** was built in the 12th century as a bastide attached to Castelnau, and it still has its central square with covered market hall and arcades; also some 15th-century houses. It is a very attractive little place, right alongside the river Cère, just 9km from the really delightful market town of St. Céré.

St. Céré is a happy little town with the Bave river washing the walls of flower-decked old houses. Built in the 9th century at an important route junction, a trading centre in the 13th century, it is still a market town for prosperous surrounding farms specialising in plums and strawberries; also a fine centre for touring and walking.

Defended by a series of castles, especially St. Laurent, whose two towers look down a steep hill to the old brown-tiled roofs, St. Céré escaped remarkably from the ravages of wars. It still has a medieval air, especially in the photogenic place du Mercadiel and in rue Paramelle, with wooden houses, 12th-century windows and 15th–16th-century mansions.

St. Laurent towers (12th and 15th centuries) were the home from 1945 until his death in 1966 of artist Jean Lurçat, who revived and revolutionised the art of tapestry. Here he designed his richly coloured tapestries and his ceramics, including his controversial but magnificent series of tapestries in Angers on the Loire called 'Song of the World', depicting a modern view of life, the world and its possible ending designed after he had seen the medieval tapestry series 'The Apocalypse' in the same city. There is a Jean Lurçat museum of his work in Angers, and a Jean Lurçat Cultural Centre with a tapestry museum in Aubusson in the Uppe Creuze Valley. And now his widow has opened a charming museum of his work in St. Laurent towers, with a short film. You can also

St. Peter's church, Beaulieu-sur-Dordogne, was built by monks in the 12th century.

Long view from St. Médard-de-Presque to the castle of Castelnau over Bave river.

see some of his best ceramics in the bar of the Casino in St. Céré, with a glass in your hand. You can see his famous tapestry of a puffed-up cock in a coat of many colours in Hôtel Coq Arlequin which Gérard Bizat's family have kept over 100 years. Gérard was himself a painter and close friend of Lurçat. Alas, it is now a bed and breakfast hotel. The superb regional Bizat dishes are served 2km away at Grill du Coq Arlequin beside a swimming pool.

St. Céré has a delightful Satur-day market taking up the main square

and the whole centre of the little town.

Three kilometres out of town is the romantic, sad *Château de Montal*, the phoenix castle. Jeanne de Balsac d'Entragues built it in 1534, hiring the greatest builders, craftsmen and artists. She was a widow and she built this country mansion on the site of a feudal fort as a present for her eldest son Robert, who was away in Italy fighting with Francis I.

The mansion was finished. The mother waited, watching from a high

Old Quercy doorway at St. Médard-de-Presque

window for her son's return. Alas, only his body returned. Jeanne had the high window blocked up and beneath it carved 'Hope No More'.

Montal became uninhabitable during the Revolution. In 1879 an asset-stripper bought it and sold it off in lots, some of the stone going to Paris. The masterpieces were dispersed. In 1908 a new owner M. Fenaille, bought what was left and restored it. He found and bought at inflated prices all the treasures and artistic pieces, from private collections and museums all over the world. One stone doorway was missing. So he commissioned the great sculptor Rodin to make another. When all was complete, he gave it in 1913 to the nation.

The Bave is a very pleasant little river and the D30 road west from St. Céré is rewarding for scenery. You can turn off just past Montal to the **Grotte de Presque**, a series of caves, chambers and galleries going 350m into rock. The stalagmite piles are in strange shapes and some are wonder-

105

fully slender and white, but it is not quite in the same underground class as nearby Gouffre de Padirac.

Another road left from D30, the D38, follows the lovely valley of the little Autoire river, lined with walnut and poplar trees and old houses with dovecots, almost a symbol of old Quercy (see box).

The village of **Autoire** is absolutely delightful. In its old streets you see half-timbered and old corbelled houses, turreted villas and old manors, with fountains in the squares. From a terrace by the church you can see the amphitheatre of rocks (**Cirque d'Autoire**) which you can reach by driving on to a car park and taking a pathway overlooking a series of waterfalls in the river. Cross the bridge and climb the steep rock path for a fine view of the amphitheatre, the river and the village. Autoire is definitely a place to see.

You can go straight on from the Cirque to Padirac, but for scenery and interest it is better to return to D30, then turn off on the delightful D118 to **Loubressac**, a bastide on a rocky spur overlooking the Bave river. It is an enchanting little town of narrow alleys winding between old houses, a fine tree-shaded square where you can park to wander on foot, and a 15th-century manor house, called a château, at the end of the spur, over-looking the junction of three valleys. Alas, it is no longer open — a pity, for it has some beautiful Louis XIII and Revolutionary period furniture.

Gouffre de Padirac (Padirac Chasm) has been called 'The Underground

The phoenix Château de Montal near St. Céré was built for a soldier who never saw it.

Quercy Dovecots and Country Houses

Usually dovecots in Quercy were built separately from the house and, although there was great variety in their design, most of them stood for good reason on square stone pillars well above the ground. The pigeons were kept not only for food but for their manure, which fell from the perches to the ground below and was important for manuring the land. When a father died and the property was divided between the children, they would take equal shares of the pigeon manure. These dovecots were still built until the mid-19th century. Quercy country houses were built with living rooms on the first floor, over a ground-floor space used for sheltering sheep, with the top floor or attic used for drying tobacco. On smallholdings divided into smaller units each generation, space was too precious to build separate barns.

Wonderland' and has been a tourist centre for so long that it is becoming fashionable for the snobbier French travel and guide writers to sneer at it as 'commercialised' and describe its wonders with no enthusiasm. One guide dismissed it as 'a great pot hole'. You must judge for youself. But we have found that even people who are left cold physically and mentally by caves have found Padirac beautiful and awesome and have gone far out of their way to return. You may have to travel through the caves with crowds for company in tourist season, but that will not destroy the sense of wonderment at the way an underground river has, over millions of years, cut a series of chambers and passages, nor the enchantment of sailing in a great flat-bottomed boat over the supremely translucent waters of the river with the spectacular and beautiful great cavern, Salle du Grand Dôme, at the end. Though part of the journey down to the

Dovecots were built in Quercy farms not only to provide pigeon meat but manure for the land.

107

*Loubressac — a bastide perched high on a
rocky spur overlooking the Bave valley*

St. Amadour

Who *was* St. Amadour, the mystery hermit who gave his name to Rocamadour? Frankly, no one knows. The name is believed to have come from the old language of the south, langue d'Oc, as 'roc amator' (rock lover), which became Rocamadour. The history is pretty vague. A 12th-century chronicler reported that in 1166 a local man asked to be buried beneath the threshold of the Chapel of the virgin, which, it seems, was already there. When the grave was dug, they found the body of a man. The corpse was placed near the altar and soon miracles began to happen.

Some said that the body was of an Egyptian hermit. Another theory was that it was St. Sylvanus. Then in the 15th century it was decided that the body was of Zaccheus, the publican disciple of Jesus and husband of St. Veronica. They began to preach the gospel in Palestine after Christ's death, but had to flee and the story was that they came to this area. When his wife died, Zaccheus retired to this rock to live as a hermit. The rock was his shelter, where he carved an oratory and was buried beneath it. The Chapelle Miraculeuse was built on the spot. When Henry Courtmantel robbed the treasure from the chapel, he took the great iron sword which hangs again above the door, supposed to be 'Durandel' the sword of Roland. He sold it. The chapel was crushed in 1476 by a rock fall. The one you see now was rebuilt last century. It has many votive offerings inside, such as crutches, swords, chains, banners. But most interesting is the bell hanging from the roof, believed to date from the 9th century. This is said to ring out of its own accord when a miracle is going to happen. One of the first to kneel before the virgin was Henry Plantagenet, Henry II of England, who was reported to have been miraculously cured. It is not recorded if the bell rang for him, but it did ring in warning when his son looted the chapel, which put young Henry in such a state that he fled to Martel in fear and died in penitence lying on a bed of cinders.

The statue of the Miraculous Virgin (the Black Madonna), with Jesus on her knee, is above the altar. It is believed by experts to be from the 9th century.

caverns is by lift and lifts return you to the top, there are steps to negotiate on the way down and about 1,300m of walking to do, including some slopes, as well as the 700m boat journey. The river is 103m below ground level.

The chasm was known certainly in the Hundred Years' War, when it was used as a refuge by local people, as it was in the Wars of Religion, but it seems that one year's violent flooding at the end of the 19th century opened up easier routes between the galleries — passages first discovered in 1889, by the speleologist E.A. Martel, who headed several expeditions. He found the Salle du Grand Dôme, which was opened to the public in 1890. Today expeditions still explore the river. By fluorescent colouring of the water it has been shown that the river does come above ground at the Cirque de Montvalent to the north-west by the Dordogne.

Locally it is well kown that the actual hole, the chasm, leading to the river was made by Satan himself. St. Martin, riding his mule on a soul-saving tour, met Satan, who was on his way to Hell with a whole sackful of human souls. Satan scoffed at the Saint's lowly transport and told him that he could have the sack of souls if he and his mule could cross an obstacle he would create. St. Martin took him on. The Devil dug his heel in the ground and made the hole. The athletic mule took his saintly jockey clear over it — 100m — a feat worthy of any Olympic showjumping horse. Satan left his souls and returned to Hell through the hole he had made.

Alvignac is a very pleasant place, a little spa with waters prescribed for disorders of the liver and digestion. It is a nice quiet centre for seeing the many sights around here, a much better place to stay than crowded Rocamadour.

When the charming Alice Vayssouze ran Alvignac's Grand Hotel Palladium, it was one of the best hotels to stay in the Dordogne. An excellent cook herself, she taught a string of talented young chefs who became well known. Now it is an hotel school whose pupils vary in ability. It is more formal and has lost atmosphere. But its rooms in the modern wing are very comfortable and it has a plesasant garden and swimming pool. The little clean one-star Nouvel hotel has splendid regional dishes.

Rocamadour, the spectacular city on a cliffside, grew from a hermit's cave to become a city of holy pilgrimage and now a world-renowned tourist centre.

Gramat to the south is at the eastern end of the Causse de Gramat, a wild high limestone plateau joining the Dordogne valley to the valleys of the Lot and Célé. It has an average height above sea-level of 350m. Gramat, capital of the area, has several fairs where sheep, nuts and truffles are sold. If you are there on a Thursday afternoon between mid June and mid September, you can to to an unusual holiday show — a display of dog handling at the French Police Training Centre for Handlers and Dogs. Take the little D14 south and you find **Parc de Vision**, a 40-hectare zoo and botanical park, with animals (mainly European) living in semi-captivity in their own natural environment (open daily). The botanical park is still growing.

Just above Rocamadour on D36 near l'Hospitalet is another wild animal reserve, **Forêt des Singes**, where 150

111

Barbary apes, natives of North Africa and an endangered species, roam freely in 11 hectares of woods (open 1st April–early November).

Rocamadour is ostentatiously magnificent. It is one tourist cliché which lives up to its reputation and publicity. Despite the inevitable souvenir shops, the competing restaurants, the crowds, it keeps its medieval appearance and much of its old atmosphere and splendour. Clamped to a 150m rock face, it is seen best from l'Hospitalet above it, an old hamlet with a fortified gate and the ruins of a hospital which gave bed and succour to medieval pilgrims. View it when the morning sun is on the rocks or lit up at night when it turns into a fairy city. You will never forget it.

From l'Hospitalet terrace you can look down on the outline of this extraordinary village, from the castle ramparts to the church buildings, hotels and houses to the gorge below where the river Alzou winds through fields. From the castle the town works its way down through a maze of churches, old houses, towers, oratories and rocks to the main road of the town, still high above the river valley. Rocamadour was founded by a recluse who built an oratory in the rock (see box) and pilgrims used to climb the 216 steps to the ecclesiastical city on their knees and in chains to plead forgiveness for their sins. They would kneel before the altar to the Black Virgin while the priest recited prayers and removed the chains. The priest gave the penitent a certificate and a lead image of the Virgin. Many of them needed the certificate, for they had been sentenced to make the pilgrimage by an Ecclesiastical tribunal and if they could not come back with proof of their pilgrim-

age they were in real trouble. This was particularly true of the Albigensian 'heretics' — the few who had not been put to the sword or burned down with buildings by Simon de Montfort. The pilgrims were indeed a mixed bunch, from thieves and murderers to Kings and powerful rulers — but perhaps there was not all that much difference between them in the Middle Ages.

Although it was fortified, the town was so rich that inevitably it was sacked by both English and French soldiers in the Hundred Years' War, not to mention the freelance French barons and their private armies, who were in it for the loot. Henry Courtmantel, in revolt against his father Henry II of England, plundered the church treasure to pay his army in 1183 and died in remorse. The Protestant Captain Bessonies seized the town, desecrated it and laid much waste, though the Virgin and the belfry escaped. The abbey remained empty until shut down completely in the Revolution. The pilgrimages were revived last century by the Bishops of Cahors, the churches restored. Today, very few indeed go up on their knees, but some bow the knee at every step. It might be unwise even to walk up the steps soon after a typical meal in one of the restaurants that abound in the main street. This street did survive the troubles. The gate at the end, Porte du Figuier, was a town gate in the 13th century and the town hall is a restored 15th-century Maison des Frères of the abbey. Now it contains some fine tapestries of Causse flora and fauna by Jean Lurçat, including one enormous work. (Open daily from 1st April to 30th September.) The street is crammed with souvenir shops, ice cream parlours, cafés, restaurants and the odd boutique. In the Middle

Rocamadour from the top at l'Hospitalet — the best view

Ages it would have been souvenir shops, pie shops, bakeries and inns, for there were always those in business to relieve pilgrims of their money.

The castle at the top is mainly from the last century, beside a 14th-century fort. From ramparts above a sheer drop you get a magnificent panoramic view of Rocamadour and the plateau beyond.

The tiny place St. Amadour (le Parvis des Églises) packs in seven churches, including Chapelle Miraculeuse — the Chapel of Our Lady, where the hermit is believed to have hollowed out his oratory (see box). Past the town hall in the main street below you pass through the 13th-century gate Porte Hugon, then come to Porte Basse, an attractive area where tiny houses are packed down the slope to the banks of the river.

It is a most attractive valley and you get a good view of Rocamadour from below by taking D32 to Couzou. Turn on to D39 which takes you just as attractively to the N20. Even this busy road passes through beautiful scenery

113

at this stage. Over the main road and 10km westwards is **Gourdon**, a delightful old market town on the borders of Quercy and Périgord but technically in Lot, not the Dordogne. It rises in tiers up a hill where once a castle stood, and from the terrace you can see all around you the wooded Bouriane countryside. The stonework of the old buildings has been cleaned, as in Sarlat, and it all looks bright now but not so old and dignified. The most pleasant square includes the 17th-century town hall overlooking covered arcades.

La Bouriane country to the south is a delightful secretive land with meadows, streams and woods enfolded in hills and hollows. Most people rush past it on the N20.

Superb early 17th-century doorway in the fine old town of Gourdon.

Gambetta

There is still a rue Gambetta in most larger French towns, which shows that the French have more respect for 19th-century statesmen than most other countries have.

Léon Gambetta was born in Cahors in 1838, son of a grocer of Genoese–Jewish extraction. As a young man he had a passion for the sea, but then he went as a student to watch a court case and became enthralled with the drama of the courtoom. In 1856 he left Cahors to enrol in the Paris Law Faculty. He had great courtroom success defending critics of Napoléon III's régime and was elected Deputy for Belleville in 1869. When Napoléon III surrendered to the Prussians at Sedan, Gambetta was one of the proclaimers of the Republic (4th September 1879). He became Minister of the Interior in the Government of National Defence. But Paris fell, so he escaped in a balloon to Tours and became virtual dictator of France. He called up army after army, and had a few successes but the might of the Prussian armies defeated his partly trained and amateurly led troops. He moved his Government to Bordeaux and there issued a decree disfranchising all members of royal dynasties, but he was defeated by Parisians, resigned and fled to Spain in 1871.

He was soon elected back into the Assembly by no fewer than ten départements, became leader of the advanced Republicans and formulated the Republican programme, which included such radical ideas as separation of the Church and State, liberty of the press and of meeting, free and compulsory public education, and removal of laws against trade unions.

In the election of 1881, Gambetta's party, the republican Union, was the strongest group in the Chamber, with over 200 members. But Grévy, the Republican President, disliked him and his policies and kept him out of office. He was a volatile man and the less-radical Republicans called him 'fou furieux' (raving mad). He was vastly more gifted than any of them, but they thought him dangerous and dictatorial. At last he did become prime minister in 1881 but it was an anti-climax, for only lesser-lights of the Republican cause would serve with him. He started by trying to bring in a radical change in elections. France used the single constituency system, like Britain, in those days. He wanted the list system, with voting on a departmental basis. The Chamber rejected the bill. He resigned immediately, three months after taking office. He died in the same year 1882 of an accidental wound in the hand which turned septic. He was 44.

Overleaf: *Gourdon rises in tiers up a rocky hillside*

Hotels and Restaurants

A = very expensive, B = expensive, C = moderately expensive, D = moderate, E = inexpensive.

ALVIGNAC — 46500 Gramat Nouvel Hôtel on D673 (65.33.60.30). Modern, clean, good value. Meals D–E; rooms E. Open 1st Mar–mid Dec.
Grand Hôtel Palladium on D673 (65.33.60.23). Efficient hotel school. Garden, pool; restful. Open 1st May–mid Oct. Meals C–E; rooms D.

CARENNAC — 46110 Vayrac Auberge du Vieux Quercy (65.38.69.00). Two chimney Logis. Shut mid Nov–mid Feb. Meals C–E; rooms E.

GRAMAT — 46500 Lot Lion d'or, 8 pl République (65.38.73.18). Old hotel cleverly renovated. Superb cooking of best local ingredients; old Quercy country recipes. Super Cahors wine. Highly recommended. Meals C–E; rooms D.

LACAPELLE-MARIVAL — 46120 Lot La Terrasse (65.40.80.07). Eric Bizat (ex Coq Arlequin) is a talented young chef. Good value. Closed 2nd Jan–15 Mar. Meals C–E. Rooms D–E.

LACAVE — 46200 Lot Château la Treyne (65.32.66.66). Superb river views, delightful furnishings by the owner Michèle Gombert. French-style gardens; outstanding chef Laurent Clément from Moulin de l'Abbaye (Brantôme). Expensive. Open Easter–15th Nov. Meals B–C. Rooms A–B.

MARTEL — 46600 Lot Turenne Hôtel (Restaurant la Quercy), av Jean-Lavayssière (65.37.30.30). Attractive stone inn; bedrooms spacious, comfortable. Campastie family have cooked here since 1856. Superb truffle soufflé. Meals C–E; rooms D–E.

PADIRAC — 46500 Gramat Padirac Hôtel, Gouffre de Padirac (65.33.64.23). Simple, cheap. Ultra-cheap first menu. Open end Mar–mid Oct. Meals D–E; rooms E.

PAYRAC — 46350 Lot Hostellerie de la Paix (65.37.90.37). Attractive old post inn, now Logis, with 3 chimneys for cooking. Open 20th Feb–31st Dec. Meals D–E. Rooms C–E.

ROCAMADOUR — 46500 Gramat Ste. Marie Hôtel, pl des Shenais (65.33.63.07). Renovated. Perched on rock-face with lovely views. Some rooms in annexe. Regional cooking. Open end Mar–early Oct. Meals C–E; rooms D–E.
Beau Site et Notre-Dame (Restaurant Jean de Valon), rue Roland Lepreux (65.33.63.08). Superb terrace view, especially at night. Good regional cooking. Open end March–mid Nov. Meals C–E; rooms C–E.
Panoramic, route du Château, l'Hospitalet (65.33.63.06). Little family hotel with lovely views. Good value. Open mid Feb–mid Nov. Meals C–E; rooms D–E.
Château de Roumégouse (near Rignac, 4.5km north-east of Rocamadour by N140 and D20) (65.33.63.81). Relais et Châteaux hotel in lovely neo-Gothic château with pointed tower, above Causse de Gramat. Used by resistance in World War II. Best regional cooking. Open 1st Apr–2nd Nov. Meals B–D; rooms A–D.

ST. CÉRÉ — 46400 Lot Les Trois Soleils de Montal, 3km W St. Jean Lespinasse (65.38.20.61). Charming new country hotel owned by Bizat family from Coq Arlequin in St. Céré. Excellent. Good friendly service. Very good cooking, Rooms B–C. Meals C–D.
Ric (2km south, by D48, at St. Vincent-du-Pendit) (65.38.04.08). Personalised cooking by young patron. Elegant house in woods. Meals C–E. Rooms D.

7
Cahors and Eastwards

Cahors is in a superb position within a loop of the Lot river, which almost meets in a circle, and backed by bare wild hills where once peasants fought to grow vines. Of the three bridges across which you can enter it, Pont Valentré is one of the most beautiful in France.

To see the town in its full setting you must take to the hills. Coming in from

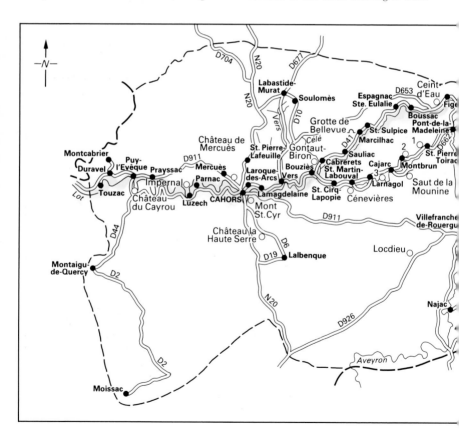

the north on N20, 3km after St. Pierre-Lafeuille, take the little V10 left running along the top of the slopes. Suddenly, you will see Cahors beneath you, stepped in terraces up the hill from the loop in the river — towers, belfries, old houses and bridges. You can get another fine view by crossing the river by Louis-Philippe bridge to the south of the town, left on D6, then left again by foot on a steep path to Mont St. Cyr, where there is a viewing table. You can see clearly how boulevard Gambetta cuts Cahors in two — the old and new towns. You can see the shape of the Valentré bridge, too.

Valentré was built across the Lot in

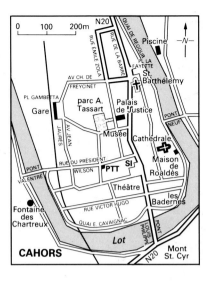

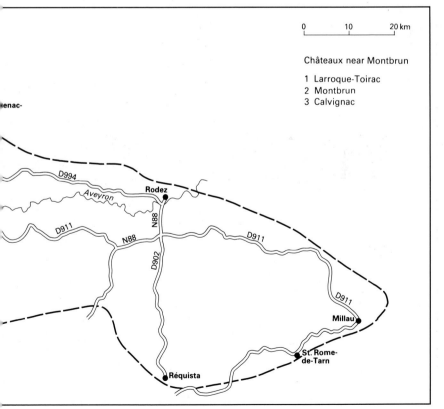

Châteaux near Montbrun

1 Larroque-Toirac
2 Montbrun
3 Calvignac

1308 and is a wonderful example of medieval military architecture. Its three square pointed towers rising 40m above the river have crenellated parapets and battlements. The centre tower was originally a look-out post and the others had gates and portcullises. It was such an effective fort that neither the English in the Hundred Years' War nor Henry of Navarre when besieging Cahors in the Wars of Religion in 1580 thought it worth attacking. Legend has it that the Devil himself helped to finish it on time. He agreed to bring all the materials necessary to the site in return for the architect's soul. When the bridge was nearly finished, the architect told the Devil to bring him water in a sieve. He tried several times but not surprisingly failed. In revenge he broke off the top stone of the central tower. Every time the stone was replaced, it fell off. Then in 1879 during restoration the stone was fixed really firmly — with a carving on it of the Devil trying to dislodge it. The central tower is open to visitors from 1st July to 31st August.

Cahors grew around a spring where the Gauls and Romans worshipped. You can reach it by crossing Valentré bridge. It is now called Fontaine des Chartreux and still supplies water for the town. The Romans built a town with temples, baths and a theatre.

In the 13th century Cahors became a powerful commercial and financial city, mainly because Lombard bankers moved in. It was one of the great banking centres of Europe, lending money to kings and popes.

When the English took nearly all the towns of Quercy at the beginning of

Le Pont Valentré at Cahors is the most beautiful fortified medieval bridge in France

the Hundred Years' War, Cahors held out, although the Black Death wiped out many of its people. But under the Treaty of Brétigny in 1360 the French king ceded Cahors to the English. The consuls of Cahors refused to give up the keys until the king ordered them. 'We are not abandoning the king — the king is abandoning us to foreigners,' they said. The English held the city until 1450. Many French left. But one lasting good came out of it for the people of Cahors. The English acquired a strong taste for Cahors wine, which has lasted right through the times when the French were not very interested in it up until today.

It was during this war in the 13th and 14th centuries that the cathedral of St. Etienne was fortified. The church was begun at the end of the 11th century and is a rather-muddled mixture of styles. The finest features are the Romanesque door, now on the north side, and the 16th-century Flamboyant-style cloisters, restored after considerable damage. The door was moved from the west to the north side during the 13th-century alterations. The tympanum is splendid — panels showing the Ascension with surrounding sculptures of the life and martyrdom of St. Stephen (St. Étienne). In one corner of the cloisters is a very attractive statue of the Virgin with long plaited hair.

The main street of Cahors, the boulevard Gambetta, which was named after the 19th-century statesman born here (see p. 115) and which cuts the attractive and interesting old town to the east from the friendly but less-interesting newer town, was once the main road, the N20, which now skirts the town. Traffic can still be formidable at rush hours. The south-east section of the old town is particularly attractive and is being well restored. Called les Badernes, it was the commercial centre in the heydays of the 13th century. It is lively and pretty. On the quai Champollion near the cathedral, Maison de Roaldès is a 15th-century mansion named for the 17th-century owners, a distinguished Quercy family, but often called Henry IV's house because he is said to have lived here while besieging Cahors. It has two contrasting façades, one with mullioned windows and doors, a rose window and the typical decorative style of old Quercy, the other with timber framing and a balcony below a large round tower.

The north of the old town, Soubirous, was where the fighting between the Catholics and Henry's Protestant forces took place. Here now stands the mostly 16th-century church of St. Barthélemy, much rebuilt over the centuries. It has a fine bell-tower and its façade is pleasant but inside are some odd decorations. The modern font in the first chapel has enamelling showing Pope John XXII. He was born in 1249 near the church, was baptised here and was probably responsible for the tradition of the Popes having the red wine of Cahors for communion. He was not a nice man. Alleging sorcery, he had the Bishop of Cahors flayed and torn apart by wild horses. Small wonder that the local people are prouder of Gambetta, who has pride of place in the Musée Municipal in the old bishop's palace (open 2nd May–31st October). But it is difficult to get excited about the exhibits of his bust, drawings and signed papers. The ceramic collection is more interesting.

Along D911 to the north-west of Cahors (7km) is a stunning castle, **Châ-**

Château de Mercuès near Cahors, first built in the 13th century, is now a luxury hotel famous for local wines.

teau de Mercuès, with four dunce's-hat turrets. It is 15th-century and was the bishop's palace for centuries. It was made into a delightful but expensive hotel by wine-maker and négociant Georges Vigouroux, who uses the caves in the huge park to mature and store wine and gives his guests free tastings.

Farther along the D911 you reach **Prayssac**, an important wine town; then, still on the D911, beside the very pleasant old Bellevue hotel which locals use, is an esplanade from which there are magnificent views of the snaking river way below and an attractive suspension bridge. A steep road takes you down to the delightful little town of **Puy-l'Evêque** snuggling by the river — very much a wine town. Old houses in golden stone rise in tiers to the church, once part of the town's defences, and the keep, all that remains of the old bishop's castle.

The nicest way back to Cahors from Puy-l'Evêque, a lovely route, is to cross the suspension bridge to the south side of the river and take D44 left, then D8 which runs, often, right alongside the river. But first, take little D28 before the bridge to see the beautiful **Château de Cayrou**, where the Jouffreau family make the best Cahors wine, which you can taste (see p. 22). They bought the property in 1971 from Comte Henri de Montpezat, of one of the great old families of Quercy. He had married in 1967 Princess Margarethe of Denmark and since she became Queen he has been called Prince Henrik. She is an archaeologist, educated at the Universities of Copenhagen, Aarhus, Cambridge, the Sorbonne in Paris and the London School of Economics.

The D8 reaches the little town of **Luzech**, nearly encircled by a loop in the Lot river. It has kept its medieval character with the square keep of the ancient castle looking down on old houses in alleys. In 1118 Richard Coeur de Lion held the castle. The English tried to take the town often in the Hundred Years' War but the castle held out, and the Catholics held it successfully against the Protestants in the Religious Wars. The Impernal hill has been inhabited since prehistoric times. Excavations have revealed walls and traces of buildings of Roman and Gaulish period.

A diversion on D23 following a river loop takes you to **Parnac**, where the Wine-Growers Co-operative Caves offer tastings (see p. 22). Rejoining D8, you can follow it to Cahors.

Southwards from these roads mentioned is a maze of little roads through farming villages and hamlets where you will see very few tourists indeed, all the way to Moissac and Montauban. The very attractive D2 road can be picked up at Montaigu-de-Quercy, south-west of Puy-l'Evêque, to near Moissac over the border in Tarn-et-Garonne.

Some of the best country of all this area, wild and sparsely inhabited, is to the north and east of Cahors. The D653 runs eastward alongside the Lot, then turns north at Vers alongside the Vers. After 8km take the little D32 left to **Labastide-Murat**. This is a delightful run, climbing to one of the highest points on the Gramat Causse. The town changed its name from Labastide-Fortunière in honour of the local man, Jean Murat, whom Napoléon made Marshal of the Empire, Grand Duke of Berg and King of Naples after displays of fanatical bravery on battlefields from Egypt to Austria, and after he married Napoléon's sister Caroline. In the retreat from Moscow, he commanded the French army after Napoléon left it. When the Bourbons returned in 1815, he tried to recapture his 'kingdom' of Naples but was taken prisoner and shot. The little inn kept by his family, where he was born, is now a Murat museum (open 1st July to 15th September) and is interesting because it is a genuine 18th-century inn saloon and kitchen. The château which he had built for his brother André is just outside the town. The more modern local inn used to be called 'Auberge du Roi de Naples' until very recently. Murat's son Napoléon Archille fled to the US, settled in Florida, married Washington's niece, and wrote a book on American Government. Labastide-Murat has important fairs. At **Soulomès**,

Puy-l'Evêque — from the terrace beside the inn are superb views of the snaking Lot river

on the D17, 3km south-east, some very interesting 14th-century frescoes have been uncovered in the Gothic church, once part of a priory, including one of doubting St. Thomas looking very surprised. Just past the village you see fine views of the Causse.

Back at Vers, the beautiful D662 road alongside the Lot takes you to some of the great treasures of this part of France. At **Bouziès**, high cliffs are riddled with caves used by prehistoric families. One, called Château des Anglais, has a castellated wall built by the English in the Hundred Years' War to fortify it. From here there are two beautiful routes, as rewarding as each other. The left-hand route on D41

follows the little Célé river valley, called in France the Valley of Paradise. The road is at first cut between the poplar-lined river bank and a cliff-face like a wall which sometimes overhangs the road. **Cabrerets** is a very pleasant little village. You can see it best by crossing the bridge to the other bank. Here another little river, the Sagne, meets the Célé, and overlooking both is the formidable **Gontaut-Biron** château, with a big corner tower and a balustraded terrace which overhangs the road 25m above it. You cannot, alas, visit the castle, but it is in a fine state of repair.

Three kilometres up D13 and D198 is **Grotte du Pech-Merle** (Pech-Merle cave), extremely important to students of prehistory and interesting to all of us. It may have been some sort of temple to the people 20,000 years ago, but it was 'lost' and rediscovered only in 1922. Cabrerets' priest, Abbé Lemozi, was a student of prehistory and a cave-explorer who made many discoveries in the area. His talks so inspired two 14-year-old schoolboys that they decided to explore a small hole known to have been used as a hiding place in the Revolution. The boys pressed on for several hours crawling along a narrow slimy trench sometimes blocked by limestone. They came finally into a chamber decorated by wonderful wall paintings and carvings.

The abbé then explored the cave expertly, realised that it was an underground temple, and soon it was opened to the public. In 1949 further exploration revealed a new chamber through which prehistoric men had entered the cave. You can now walk along vast chambers joined through wide openings and along galleries for 1,600m. It is open from Palm Sunday to 1st November. In the hall of the Broken Column are black outline drawings of bisons and mammoths in a frieze 7m long. Then comes the Galerie des Peintures (the Picture Gallery). On one wall are outlines of two horses, dotted, odd signs and outlined hand prints, made by stencilling around hands placed flat on the wall. Among other decorations are female figures outlined on a ceiling. Prehistoric footprints in wet clay are petrified for us to see. There are bones of cave-bears and the roots of an oak tree which bored down to find moisture.

The Amedée-Lemozi museum (Palm Sunday–1st November) is a research centre with attractive displays of tools, bones, utensils, arms and art works from 160 different prehistoric sites. There are colour photographs of decorated caves in Quercy and a film on paleolithic art.

Just after Cabrerets near the D41 road is the very attractive **Fontaine de la Pescalerie**. Beside an ivy-covered mill, half hidden by foliage, a lovely waterfalls pours out of the rock wall — the surfacing of an underground river that has cut its way right through the Gramat Causse. Nearby is a delightful 18th century manor called La Pescalerie, a private house now but for years a place of joy, rest, good food and good company to our readers and 'Paradise on Earth' to a distinguished French travel guide — an hotel run by two delightful doctors Hélène Combette and Roger Belcour, surgeon in Cahors by day, hotel sommelier by night and expert on Cahors wine.

D41 next dives through a tunnel, then the valley widens out. At **Sauliac** the houses cling to a fearsome cliff with openings to fortified caves used for centuries as war refuges. The fit climbed ropes to reach them, the rest were hoisted in baskets. So were the farm animals, for beyond the village the valley becomes pasture and arable land.

At **Marcilhac**, a beautiful village, are the ruins of an historic abbey. In the 11th century it controlled the little sanctuary of Rocamadour, but took no interest and let it go to ruin. Monks from Tulle installed themselves in the sanctuary, and no one minded until the discovery in 1166 of the body of St. Amadour which brought in pilgrims and wealth. Marcilhac monks threw out the monks of Tulle. Then the Abbot of Tulle threw out the Marcilhac men and reoccupied the holy shrine. Lawsuits followed and even the pope could not decide which monks should occupy it. Finally Marcilhac was bribed to give up its claim to Rocamadour.

Marcilhac prospered until the 14th century when marauding bands of English soldiers and French 'Routiers', the mercenary bands, nearly destroyed it. It was revived as a minor abbey by the Hébrard family of St. Sulpice, who were feudal lords of the Célé valley throughout the Middle Ages, but it shut in the Revolution. Though some of the Romanesque ruins are open to the sky, there are carvings in wood and stone still visible, some dating back to the 10th century. The Gothic ruins are used as a church and contain 16th-century frescoes. Fine old houses surround it all.

A road of steeply rising hairpin bends takes you in 1½km to the hamlet of Palihès and **Grotte de Bellevue** (Cave), known for its interesting and unusually shaped concretions, some dark red due to iron oxide, others shining white calcite. Stalagmites are like white, slim candles. Hercules' Column, reaching from floor to ceiling, is 4m high and 3½m wide. There is a fine view of the village and valley from the zig-zagging road.

St. Sulpice village is built under an overhanging cliff beside a medieval castle which still belongs to the Hébrard family. The valley from here on widens into cropland and vineyards, then narrows into gorges alternately, with old farmhouses and clifftop villages. **Espagnac-Ste. Eulalie** is especially attractive. Its delightful houses

with turrets and pointed roofs surround the old priory of Notre Dame du Val Paradis. Founded by an Augustinian monk in the 12th century, the priory became a convent in 1212. Much was destroyed in the Hundred Years' War, but it was rebuilt in the 15th century. Some of it is now the village school and the priest lives in the former rooms of the abbess. Inside the 11th-century Flamboyant church are tombs from an earlier church with figures of 12th- and 13th-century knights.

After Boussac the cliffs disappear and the Célé runs to Figeac through wooded hills, past the much-restored castle of Ceint-d'Eau, 15th–16th-century with massive towers.

Figeac is a busy little town, but deserves an unhurried visit, with plenty of time to wander its old streets lined with half-timbered houses with balconies, some with coats of arms, forged ironwork and mullion windows. Much restoration is taking place. It was a Protestant stronghold in the Wars of Religion. The tourist information office is in the 13th-century Hôtel de la Monnaie (the mint). So is the museum (open all year round), known best for a room devoted to Jean-Françoise Champollion, the Orientalist born in Figeac in 1790. A brilliant linguist who had a working knowledge of Greek, Latin, Hebrew, Arabic, Chaldaen and Syrian by the age of 14, he deciphered the Rosetta Stone, a tablet found by an expedition to Rosetta in the Nile Delta of Egypt. The original of the stone is in the British Museum, but there is a moulding in Figeac's museum.

The other route from Bouziès to Figeac follows the Lot river. First cross the river at Bouziès and take the little winding D40, a very scenic road cut into the cliff to **St. Cirq-Lapopie** (pronounced St. 'Sear'). Perched on a high escarpment dropping vertically to the river banks and facing a semi-circle of cliffs, it has been a coveted strongpoint since the 8th century when the Duke of Aquitaine made it a defence stronghold. The Lapopie family owned the castle in the Middle Ages and even Richard Coeur de Lion failed to take it in 1198. In the Hundred Years' War the English failed to take it from the Lord of Cardaillac, but the castle had such potential for enemies of the French kings that in 1471 Louis XI ordered it to be demolished. Even the ruins were important enough for the Protestants to take them. Henry of Navarre had all the remaining walls knocked down. Now visitors climb the steep path from the village below for a superb view over the village, river and countryside to the wooded hills of the Gramat Causse.

The old houses in the steep narrow streets of the village built into the side of the cliff have been lovingly restored, mostly by painters or wood-craftsmen, and the whole village is a delight, though crowded with visitors in midsummer. The 15th-century church, with a squat belfry tower and round turret, is on a terrace of rock overlooking the river, with more fine views.

The 15th-century fortified church of St. Cirq-Lapopie stands on a rock terrace overlooking the Lot river.

The village was known for centuries for its craftsmen wood-turners. There are still one or two producing spigots and taps for wine and beer barrels.

Cross the river to D662 for an attractive run to St. Martin-Labouval. Beside it is the village of La Toulzanie, built right under an overhanging cliff. Cross the river again on to the D8 at **Cénevières Château**, a huge castle clinging to a rock-face (guided tours Easter to All Saints' Day). It has a 13th-century keep with secret dungeons and a stone staircase leading to a fine Renaissance gallery. Furnishings are very attractive, with 15th–16th-century Flemish and Aubusson tapestries and there are good views of the Lot valley from the terrace. Stay on the D8 to **Calvignac**, an old village perched on a spur, with good river views, then recross to D662 to Larnagol. There are more lovely views on the way to Cajarc, an attractive old village. Here it is worth a diversion over the river and along the south bank on D127 to **Saut de la Mounine** — a steep cliff with a superb view over a huge bend in the river. The legend of La Mounine's Leap is a typicaly cruel tale of the Middle Ages. The Lord of Montbrun, a castle whose ruins you can see opposite, ordered his daughter to be hurled from the top of the cliff for having a love-affair with another lord's son. The local hermit was so appalled that he dressed up a poor blind monkey (mounine) in women's clothes and threw that over. Seeing what he thought was his daughter hurtling to her death, the lord was struck by remorse. When he saw her alive, he forgave her. The legend does not say whether she forgave him, nor does it express any remorse for the blind monkey.

Return to Cajarc over the river and follow the attractive stretch of D662 to Montbrun, which rises in tiers to the ruins of **Montbrun** castle. It is in a lovely situation. The road continues to another château, **Larroque-Toirac**, a spectacular fortress clamped to a high cliff-face, originally owned by the Cardaillac family who led French resistance in Quercy against the English in the Hundred Years' War. It changed hands several times and was burned down, but rebuilt during Louis XI's reign (open early July–early September). Inside are furnishings from Louis XIII's reign to the Directorate (early 17th to early 18th centuries).

St. Pierre-Toirac, the next village, has a fortified Benedictine church built from the 11th to 14th centuries, with a massive crenellated keep. Cross the river again here to the D86, a very attractive road running alongside the river, especially after the Madeleine

bridge to Capdenac-Gare. Just north on the way to Figeac is the little village of **Capdenac-le-Haut**, up a steep hill off N140. Perched on a rock encircled by a loop of the Lot river, it still looks much like a medieval village, with its narrow streets lined with wooden houses with pointed arches. There are wonderful views from the terrace as you enter and from another near the church. The ramparts and castle are in ruins, but this was once a stronghold of great strategic importance, especially in the Hundred Years' War. In the Religious Wars it was a main Protestant stronghold, and Henry IV's great Minister, the Duke of Sully, lived in it for some years after Henry was assassinated.

The border between the départements of Lot and Aveyron runs somewhat illogically along the Lot river, for it changes banks, and although Aveyron may not be in Lot for administrative purposes, no one exploring this delightful wild country is going to stop dead at the river for that reason. This part of Aveyron is very much touring country for visitors staying anywhere near the Lower Lot Valley.

Due south of Figeac and east of Cahors is **Villefranche-de-Rouergue**, a fine example of a bastide made by Alphonse de Poitiers in 1252 from a town on the banks of the Aveyron river founded in 1099. Though its ramparts and fortified gates have gone, it still has the look of a bastide in the centre. Local silver mines ensured its medieval prosperity. Cornières Square, a cobbled, sloping market square in the very centre, is surrounded by old arcaded houses and has the massive gate-tower of the collegiate church of Notre-Dame in one corner. It is 58m high, built to rival the bell-tower of the

Figeac – a charming old town (photograph by Images Colour Library)

cathedral at Rodez when these two ambitious towns were fighting for local supremacy. The road runs beneath it. The church was built over three centuries from 1260. The richly decorated choir stalls were made by the 15th-century sculptor André Sulpice. The market is held on Thursdays.

Chapelle des Pénitents Noirs in a nearby boulevard was built in the 17th century for the Brotherhood of Black Penitents founded in 1609. It lasted until 1904. The great monument of the town is the Chartreuse St. Sauveur (open all year). A rich merchant named Vézien-Valette founded this Charter-house in 1451 and it was finished in eight years. The style is pure Gothic. During the Revolution, it was in danger of being pulled down until the local

authorities said that they needed it as a town hospital. The founder and his wife have a fine monumental tomb in the chapel. The cloister is enormous — one of the biggest in France, and had monks' cells surrounding it. But the Flamboyant Gothic small cloister is the more attractive. In the refectory is a Flamboyant Gothic pulpit from which the Bible was read aloud during meals.

Ten kilometres south-west of Ville-franche on the Quercy border is **Loc-dieu**, a Cistercian abbey converted last century into a château open July, August, not Tuesdays).

There is some beautiful country south of Villefranche, both along D922 and the little D47 which follows the Aveyron river through the rugged Gorges de l'Aveyron. The scenery

129

around **Najac** is outstandingly beautiful, with wooded hills, steep valleys and rough little switchback roads joining farmsteads and hamlets, some deserted, right alongside the border of Quercy. Few Frenchmen know this area. The spectacular ruins of the 13th century dominate the whole area of peaks, with the houses of the little town climbing uphill nearby. As you climb, dive and twist around the little roads, you get constant glimpses into the Aveyron river gorge below. The original castle was a major work of military architecture. The view from the donjon tower, plunging dizzily to the river on three sides, is not for those with vertigo. A bridge over the steep river ravine leads you soon to Belle Rive, a pleasant little hotel with views over the river valley and a weir.

Rodez, to the east of Villefranche, was the old capital of Rouergue. Built in a bend of the Aveyron river, 120m above the water, it has a fine red sandstone cathedral built over three centuries. Originally it was also part of the town's defences and it looks like it, but later an attractive Flamboyant Gothic upper section was added. Above the Flamboyant rose window is a Renaissance gable. The bell-tower, beautifully proportioned, is 87m high. The plain lower section was built in the 14th century. The three upper tiers, richly ornamented in Flamboyant–Gothic style, were added by Bishop François d'Estaing in 1526. Inside, the choir stalls are once again by André Sulpice. The nave is plain but impressive.

The Bishop's Palace opposite the cathedral's north door was largely restored last century, but still has a 17th-century staircase copied from Fontainebleau. There are fine old houses around the cathedral and south of it in place du Bourg, though the town is mostly modern.

Rodez is 630m above sea-level and has severe winter weather. It was occupied by the English from 1360 for eight years, hence the massive 14th-century Tour des Anglais east of the cathedral. The people were steadfast in resisting the English and in this century they resisted the Nazi occupation in World War II so ardently that the day before the Germans evacuated the town in August 1944, they shot 32 hostages. But they were not always so united. In the Middle Ages the people of the Bishop's cité and those of the 'bourg' ruled by the local counts disliked each other so heartily that a wall had to be built to separate them. The Saturday market is now in the bishop's part of the town, place de la Cité.

There is more splendid countryside climbing over the mountains to the south of Rodez on D902 to Réquista and the Tarn river, between this road and N88 to the west, and especially on small roads along the Tarn from Réquista to St. Rome-de-Tarn to Millau, busy industrial and tourist centre on the river Tarn, roughly where the Massif Central meets the Midi. Since the 12th century it has produced gloves, and still makes about 350,000 pairs a year, half France's production. Of equal importance these days, it is the favourite starting point for excursions to the Gorges du Tarn, the most famous and spectacular gorges in France. But that is for another book.

Hotels and Restaurants

A = very expensive, B = expensive, C = moderately expensive, D = moderate, E = inexpensive.

CABRERETS — 46330 Lot Auberge de la Sagne, route de Pech-Merle (65.31.26.62). Charming old inn; quiet. Very good value. Open 1st May–1st Oct. Meals D–E; rooms D–E.

CAHORS — 46000 Lot La Taverne, 1 rue J-B Delpech (65.35.28.66). Quercynoise dishes. Wonderful selection of Cahors wines. Meals A–E.
Terminus Hotel (La Balandre restaurant), ave. Charles-de-Freycinet (65.35.24.50). Good traditional Quercy cooking. Meals C–E; rooms D–E.
Beau Rivage (at Laroque-des-Arcs, 5km on D653) (65.35.30.58). Beautiful views over Lot river; big garden. Open 1st Apr–31 Oct. Meals B–E; rooms D.

CARDAILLAC — 46100 Figeac Chez Marcel (65.40.11.16). Charming old inn. Meals very good value indeed. Meals D–E; rooms E.

FIGEAC — 46100 Lot Des Carmes, enclos des Carmes (65.34.20.78). Modern, with pool. Excellent Quercy cooking with modern touches. Meals C–E; rooms D.

LABASTIDE-MURAT – 46240 Lot Climat de France, pl de la Mairie (65.21.18.80). Charming very cheap village inn. Meals E; rooms D–E.

MERCUÈS – 46090 Cahors Château de Mercuès (65.20.00.01). Castle made into expensive delightful hotel. Magnificent views. Wine cave in grounds. Talented chef. Open 1st Apr–30 Oct. Relais et Château hotel. Meals B–D; rooms A–B.

MONTBRUN — 46160 Lot Ferme de Montbrun (65.40.67.71). Farm restaurant, three rooms. Farm produce, light cuisine. Open Easter–1st October. Meals C–E. Rooms D–E.

NAJAC — 12270 Aveyron Belle Rive (2km north-west by D39) (65.29.73.90). Simple country hotel. Pool. Good value. Open end Mar–end Oct. Meals D–E; rooms D–E.

PUY-L'EVÊQUE — 46700 Lot Bellevue, on D911 (65.21.30.70). Truly *belle vue* of Lot river. Good value. Open 15th Mar–15th Nov. Meals C–E; rooms D–E.

RODEZ — 12000 Aveyron Hostellerie de Fontanges (4km north off D901 at Onet-le-Château 65.42.20.28). 16th century château in park. Fine views from terrace. Pool. Very pleasant. Good value. Meals C–E. Rooms C.

ST. CIRQ-LAPOPPIE — 46330 Cabrerets Auberge du Sombral (65.31.26.08). Beautifully restored old house. Open 1st Apr–mid Nov. Meals C–E; rooms D–E.

TOUZAC — 46700 Puy L'Evêque La Source Bleue (12km west of Puy-l'Evêque on D911) (65.36.52.01). 14th-century mill in countryside; peaceful. Open 1st Apr–31 Dec. Meals C–E; rooms D.

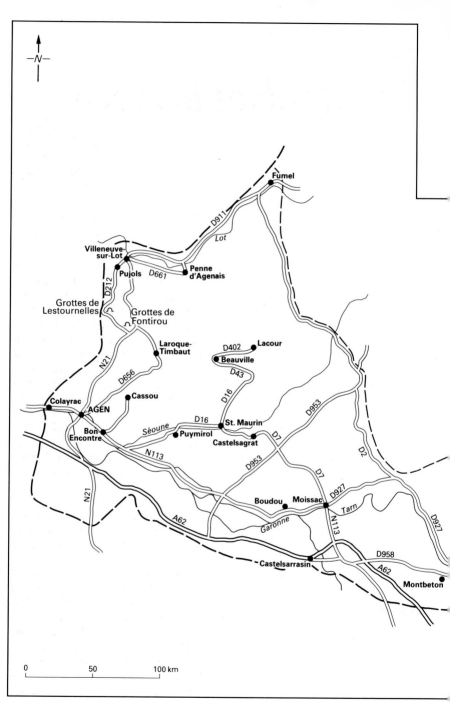

8
Montauban to Agen

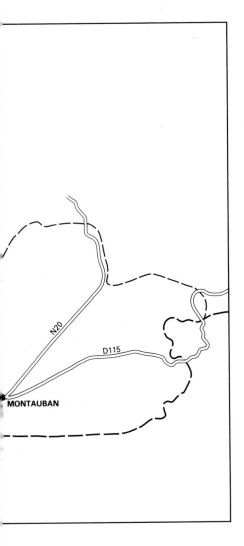

Napoléon's arbitrary decision in 1808 to split Bas-Quercy from the département of Lot, add parts of Rouergue, Gascony, and Languedoc, and create a new département called Tarn-et-Garonne, has still not been accepted by many local people, who regard the whole area as Quercy. The link with the Garonne is by way of the Tarn and Aveyron rivers, and along the low-lying riverbanks are fertile stretches of land producing fruit, cereals, vines and some tobacco, while higher ridges are used for sheep grazing and oak woods. When Algeria, Morocco and Tunisia freed themselves from France, many of the 'Pied-Noir' (French North African) farmers settled here, so not so many farmhouses were abandoned as in Lot. It is one of France's most important sheep-rearing areas, mostly the 'spectacled' sheep with very white fleece and black rings around the eyes.

Montauban has a very important and lively food market, and is a busy rail and road junction, linked by A62 motorway to Bordeaux in the northwest and Toulouse in the south, with linking motorways to Narbonne, Spain and along the Mediterranean. Industry is growing. Standing on a terrace above the Tarn, its old pink-brick buildings

133

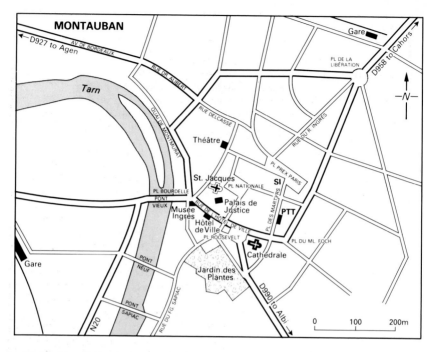

MONTAUBAN

give it a friendly bright but comfortable look. It grew from a bastide built in 1144 by the Count of Toulouse and a settlement around a Benedictine abbey, but suffered· severely for its people's religious beliefs. First it was the victim of Simon de Montfort's Albigensian persecutions. Then it became a great Protestant stronghold in the 16th-century religious wars. Henry of Navarre improved its fortifications and the Reformed churches of France held their congresses here. It was one of the four cities named for Protestant freedom of worship, and Calvinists from many countries, including Scotland, attended its Protestant Academy. But when Louis XIII came to the throne and ended freedom of worship, an army of 20,000 under the abominable Charles de Luynes was sent to bring Montauban to its knees. The people's resistance was so heroic that three major

attacks were repulsed and the siege was called off after three months. But when La Rochelle fell to Richelieu's forces, Montauban was the last Protestant stronghold left and it showed no futher resistance. Although the Protestants were given a royal pardon, Richelieu billeted his dreaded 'Dragonnades' there, troops ordered to behave with the utmost brutality to cow the citizens. The people remained staunch Protestants.

One of three bridges, Pont Vieux, was built in the 14th century at the same time as the Valentré bridge at Cahors and it was once similarly fortified. Built entirely of brick, it is 205m long, crossing the Tarn on seven arches, divided by smaller arches as floor protection. It leads to the Bishop's Palace, an impressive red brick château on the site of a castle built by England's Black Prince during the

Ingres

Born in Montauban in 1780, Jean Dominique Auguste Ingres had a very talented father who was a painter, sculptor, architect and musician. He himself was a good violinist and played most of his life, but he chose art and became not only a great painter but one of the greatest draughtsmen in French art. He made the most careful sketches even of tiny details before he started to paint a picture, sometimes sketching in the lines on his canvas, and his paintings reveal this in their pure and expressive linear perfection. He admired and was strongly influenced by the works of Raphael.

His teacher in Paris was David. Early in his career he won the Prix de Rome, went to Italy and stayed 18 years, returning several times to France. In 1826 he became Professor of Fine Arts at the Academy in Paris and recognised leader of a school of painting, but acrimonious attacks on his paintings by Paris critics made him escape to Rome in 1834 as director of the French Acadamy there. Paris rediscovered him, he was given many honours, and he returned to Paris in 1841. He was still painting at 82. He died in 1867, aged 85.

His great portraits and many of his greater works were painted in his first period in Rome. He liked painting nude women and one of the great treasures of the Louvre is his 'Odalisque', a beautiful painting of a beautiful woman reclining nude on a couch. He painted it in 1813 for Caroline, Queen of Naples and sister of Napoléon, who married Napoléon's General Murat who was given the crown of Naples. Ingres had already painted for her a sleeping nude. When Napoléon fell and Murat with him, the sleeping nude was lost but the reclining girl survived.

Hundred Years' War. When the church here was suppressed during the Revolution, the palace was bought by the town and turned into a museum in 1843. It is named after the painter and brilliant draughtsman Jean Ingres, born here in 1780, son of a painter, sculptor and architect (see box).

The most remarkable of Ingres' works here is his picture of 'Christ and the Doctors', painted when the artist was 82. It was said to be inspired by Raphael but is dull in comparison. More worthy of him is the vast 'Dream of Ossian', painted in 1812 and intended for Napoléon's bedroom in Rome — a work in monochrome.

There are paintings by his contemporaries David, Chasseriau,. Géricault and Delacroix, and his pupil Gérome, but nothing very exciting. More interesting are drawings from the nude and the 4,000 drawings he left the town which, alas, are shown in rotation and not enough at a time. His painting materials are shown and his famous violin. Students of art or art enthusiasts may, we are told, obtain permission to go through the boxes of drawings if they apply beforehand.

These paintings are all on the first floor, which has been luxuriously modernised, with comfortable armchairs for the weary. The ground floor is devoted to two other local artists — the 19th-century sculptor

THE DORDOGNE AND LOT

Antoine Bourdelle (1861–1929) and the 20th-century landscape artist Desnoyer (1894–1972). In Paris, Bourdelle has a whole museum to himself. There is his greatest work, 'Hercules Drawing his Bow'. Here in Montauban it is in plasterwork. There are some fine busts, including Beethoven, Ingres and Rodin, to whom he was chief assistant from 1893–1908. His bronze of 'Rembrandt as an Old Man' is excellent.

The furniture displayed in the second floor is more interesting than the paintings around it, but best of all is the view of the Tarn and the old bridge. The basement includes a former guardroom of the Black Prince, a good collection of local pottery and various other items including some nasty instruments of torture.

Two fine works by Bourdelle are in the town. Opposite the Ingres museum is a bronze, 'The Last Dying Century', which he composed in 1914, and on quai de Montmurat near the old bridge is the 1870 War Memorial.

A few blocks from the museum is the Church of St. Jacques, a fortified church which was declared a cathedral after the Catholics regained the town, but ceased to be so in 1739. The 13th-century octagonal belfry in red brick was built on to a square battlement tower. The present cathedral of Notre Dame is a huge Classical church with two square towers, started in 1692, finished in 1739. Inside is a well-known painting by Ingres, the 'Vow of Louis XIII', with that devout, cruel, frightened monarch offering the kingdom of France to the Virgin and the infant Jesus.

It is a pity that the old square of Montauban, place Nationale, should have been made into a car park. It looks better in the morning when a colourful market fills it. The houses around it are built of pink brick and the arcades of brick were built in the 17th century following fires which destroyed wooden market covers.

Neither of the roads to Moissac is very attractive, although the D927 does follow the Tarn most of the way, and right off this road is the beautiful D2 mentioned in Chapter 7, passing through hills and remote hamlets to lead ultimately to the D911 west of Puy-l'Evêque. **Moissac** is known for two things — its superb abbey church cloisters and chasselais dessert grapes. It is the marketing town for the fruit grown along the Tarn and Garonne rivers. The grapes are sweet, almost perfumed and have excellent flavour.

It is a wonder that any of Moissac abbey still exists. It was founded in the 7th century by Benedictine monks from St. Wandrille's Abbey near Caudebec in Normandy and was plundered by successive invaders, but St. Odon, the great Abbot of Cluny, attached it in 1047 to that rich and influential establishment which was one of the great educational centres of Europe. Moissac itself became rich and influential, establishing its own priories elsewhere, even in Catalonia. The Hundred Years' War brought English occupation twice, Simon de Montfort's troops attacked it in 1212 and pillaged it, and the Protestants damaged the sculptures in the Wars of Religion. It was pillaged again in the Revolution and secularised. During the industrial expansion of France in the middle of the last century, it faced total destruction to make way for the Bordeaux–Sète railway line, but the Beaux Arts Department stepped in just in time to save it.

The church itself is a 15th-century brick building incorporating the 11th-century belfry porch, obviously built for defence, with a watch-path. Students of religious architecture come from all over the world to see the magnificent south doorway. The tympanum over it, carved around 1100, is considered to be a masterpiece of Romanesque sculpture. It is certainly beautiful and awesome. Here is Christ in Majesty surrounded by the old men who appeared to St. Paul in his vision of the Apocalypse, and four saints — St. Matthew as a winged young man, St. Mark as a lion, St. Luke as a bull and St. John as an eagle. St. Peter, patron saint of the abbey, appears as himself.

The cloisters were finished at the end of the 11th century and truly are beautiful. Marble columns, in white, pink, green and grey, supporting the 76 arches are alternately single and double, with square supporting piers in the middle and corner of each side of the square. The ornate capitals of carved marble show biblical scenes, except a centre pier of one gallery which has a portrait of Abbot Durand de Bredon, Bishop of Toulouse, who consecrated the church in 1053. A large old cedar tree grows in the close. The cloisters are open daily except Christmas Day and New Year's Day.

Eight kilometres south across the Tarn from Moissac is **Castelsarrasin**, another important market town which started as a bastide. It spreads down to the river Garonne, which goes on to join the Tarn 5km west of Moissac. In the former Carmelite church is the tomb of Antoine de Lamothe-Cadillac, founder of Detroit. He was born across the Garonne river at St. Nicolas-de-la-Grave in 1658.

Just outside Moissac to the west a little road right off N113 leads to Boudou where there is a splendid view over both river valleys. Tiny roads north–west of Moissac, crossing the D953, lead to the well-preserved little bastide of Castelsagrat. This is an area well worth exploring, for it sees few tourists and has some fine old villages.

Castelsagrat was founded in 1270. It still has its arcaded market square with attractive old houses with round tiled roofs on all four sides, and a 14th-century church. Seven kilometres north-west is the old village of **St. Maurin** whose houses with round-tiled roofs are built in terraces among old towers left from days when this was attached to Cluny abbey. There is an old covered market. Take the very pleasing D16 northwards, then left on D43 to **Beauville**, a village on top of a ridge among orchards and vines. The arcaded street has a mixture of stone and wooden houses, and on the tip of the ridge is a Renaissance fortified farm with a machicolated tower.

The D402 eastwards has views of the Quercy hills and D7 left leads to **Lacour**, a most attractive Quercy hamlet perched on a hill. Its Romanesque church has a massive square belfry, undoubtedly built as a defensive keep for villagers when the marauding soldiers of the Hundred Years' War came this way. Lacour is in Tarn-et-Garonne, Beauville is in Lot-et-Garonne.

West of St. Maurin, also in Lot-et-Garonne, is yet another old bastide, **Puymirol**, founded in 1246 and still with some old timbered houses. It stands on a hill overlooking the valley of the little Séoune with views of the productive plains of the Agenais.

137

Prunes

Agen prunes compete with Californian to be best in the world, and France has no doubt about which wins. Tours on the Loire is famous for prunes, too, but many of the plums are imported from other districts. Originally, most Tours plums came from Damascus, hence damsons.

The grafted *prunier d'ente* trees of the Agenais produce a red, fleshy plum ideal for drying. The grafting of plum trees was brought back from the Middle East by Crusaders and it was monks who first saw the potential of plum orchards on a big scale. The Lot-et-Garonne produces 75 per cent of France's plums, mostly from north of the two rivers. Most prune orchards are planted with a type called Robe–Sergent. Though there are modern methods of drying, most plums are dried in drying rooms (like roofed but open shelves) or ovens, and these are often in the orchards.

All over France, prunes are used in many types of dishes, from meat to desserts. Long before nouvelle cuisine chefs started to serve various fruits with meat; centuries before the kiwi fruit was known in France, prunes were being used in meat dishes from Brittany to Alsace, Normandy to Provence. *Lapin aux pruneaux* (rabbit with prunes) is the great favourite here in the south-west. In Brittany, *poularde à la Rennaise* is chicken stuffed with pork and livers with prunes. They also have a *far Breton* (sweet batter) with prunes. *Noisette de porc aux pruneaux* in the Loire is loin of pork in white wine with prunes.

In Gascony there is *galette aux Pruneaux* — pancake alternately layered with a sweet prune filling, and in the Basque country, *gâteau Basque aux prunes* is a typical Basque pie filled with a thick prune purée instead of the traditional rum cream. Prunes are served in various areas as snacks wrapped in bacon, with veal and even with lamb. *Pruneaux fourrés* are one of France's most delicious confectioneries — prunes stuffed with a purée of prunes and almond paste.

Puymirol is famed these days for a chef, Michel Trama, who owns a restaurant in a lovely 13th-century house called L'Aubergade once belonging to the counts of Toulouse. His cooking has won him accolades from gourmets and gastronomic guide books all around the world. Wonderful to find one of the world's very greatest chefs in this unassuming village of 794 people in Lot-et-Garonne. The important town of Agen, 16km west, with 33,000 people, does not have a restaurant in the same class, despite being the centre of market gardening and the market town for the food from the fertile Agenais, especially the famous Agen prunes. What it does have, just outside at **Bon-Encontre**, is a most attractive hotel with restaurant, Château de St. Marcel, once the riverside residence in a pleasant park of the Count de Montesquieu, the great 18th-century writer. The drive is lined by 112 cedars, 300 years old.

Agen is a busy modern town on the Garonne, half-way between Bordeaux and Toulouse, with the A62 motorway alongside. Its railway station is important, too, and the Garonne lateral canal runs through it, crossing the Garonne river on an impressive aquaduct, 500m long with 23 arches.

Though it is very busy, Agen is a handsome town with wide avenues and the pleasant Gravier Esplanade and riverside walks. It has a rewarding museum, too. The most beautiful exhibit is a Greek marble statue discovered in 1876 near the Mas d'Agenais and named Venus du Mas. There is a fine collection of faience ceramics from contemporaries of Bernard Palissy (1510–1590), a Monpazier potter who spent his life inventing a new type of ceramic, and of paperweights from the 18th and 19th centuries.

The paintings include some fine works of Goya, including 'Caprichos' (Caprices) showing a cow and an elephant flying over a crowd of very amazed and frightened people (claimed by some critics to be the fore-runner of surrealism) and 'The Mont-golfier Balloon', showing the launching in Madrid in 1793 of a balloon by the Montgolfier brothers, who launched the first ever balloon in Paris ten years before. Some good 19th-century works include Corot's 'L'Etang de Ville d'Avray', fine landscapes by Sisley and Labasque and a Post-Impressionist collection which includes several paintings by Boudin. In the centre courtyard is a Renaissance sculpture and there is a fine spiral staircase in the Vaurs mansion. From the tower are good views of the town and the hillsides of the Agenais, with a viewing table.

The N21 north from Agen to Ville-neuve-sur-Lot has little to recommend it. Take D656 north-east, then turn left

on D110 to Laroque-Timbaut, where old houses line alleys and passages around the covered market.

D110 to the N21 is the most attractive stretch of road in this little area. Turn left for 3km down N21 then right on to the little D212. Just off to the right are **Grottes de Fontirou**, caves with pure white stalagmites and reddish-yellow concretions coloured by clay (open daily Palm Sunday to 1st November, Sundays and holidays only the rest of the year).

Turn right off D212 on to D220 to the **Grottes de Lestournelles**, caves hollowed out by underground rivers, with stalactites still forming (open daily 1st June–30th September, Sundays only for rest of year except 1st January–1st March, when they are closed). Neither of these caves compares with the great caves in the Dordogne and Lot but they are worth visiting.

This countryside of Lot-et-Garonne does not have the beauty of the Dordogne département nor the rugged majesty of the Lot, but it is most pleasantly attractive and if you wander its small side roads you find many charming old villages and hamlets which seem still to be living in a different century.

We can remember some years ago when it was difficult to believe that you were in the 20th century when you strolled among the small streets of **Villeneuve-sur-Lot**. New buildings, more traffic and many more visitors have changed it, but much of its medieval charm remains, for it has been splendidly preserved, and it is in no way a tourist museum but a business centre and busy little marketing centre for fruit and vegetables, especially the *prunier d'ente* — the grafted plum which is dried to make the excellent Agen prunes. It has good markets on Tuesdays and Saturdays.

Villeneuve spreads along the banks of the Lot. It was founded as a bastide by that bastide-enthusiast Alphonse de Poitiers, brother of Louis IX, in 1264, but these bastides changed hands frequently and Villeneuve soon fell to the English. The 13th-century bridge which the English built is still there, from which are good views of the quay and the old houses.

All that remains of the old bastide ramparts are two gates, the three-storey Porte de Pujols and the Porte de Paris. Both were built of stone and brick and topped by battlements and crenellations. As you walk around the town you find reminders of its past in the old houses, tiny streets and towers.

Villeneuve is a most pleasant little town going about its own business, where visitors are welcome but not a great deal is done to lure them. The tourist target is the little old village of Pujols on the south-west edge of the town, and from the hill where it stands you can get one of the best views of Villeneuve.

Pujols is a delightful old walled village, if somewhat decayed. You can enter through a passageway beneath the belfry tower of St. Nicolas church and right away you are among tight-packed houses inside its 13th-century ramparts. There are still many timbered houses with porch roofs and fine Renaissance houses. It also has the best-known restaurant in this area — La Toque Blanche. It is in a modern block opposite the village and is very expensive, but Bernard Lebrun's cooking is outstanding and his dishes largely old-fashioned regional with fine old sauces, making full use of fresh ingredients from Villeneuve market.

From Villeneuve, take the D661 for 8km east to **Penne-d'Agenais**, another fortified village, built by the English. Richard Coeur de Lion fortified it, and a fountain and the Richard gate are left to remind us. Penne was in ruins and almost deserted until restoration started in the 1950s. Now it is a great tourist draw. 16th-century houses near the Porte de Ville entrance to the village and older flower-decked houses in the lanes of the upper town have all been skilfully renovated. The basilica, Notre Dame de Peyragude, is in Romanesque–Byzantine style, but is modern. It is crowded with pilgrims in May and June, others make for the Sunday morning market. A very good reason for visiting Penne on any clear day is the remarkable view, stretching right along the Lot river from Ville-neuve to Fumel, in the north-east, on the road to Cahors. and Penne d'Agenais is, in fact, on D911, the wine road through Puy-l'Evêque to Cahors.

Hotels and Restaurants

A = very expensive, B = expensive, C = moderately expensive, D = moderate, E = inexpensive.

AGEN — 47000 Lot-et-Garonne Château de St. Marcel (at Bon-Encontre — 47240 Lot-et-Garonne — 5km east of Agen) (53.96.61.30) (see p. 138). Riverside château in park. Delightful. Meals C–D; rooms A–C.
La Table de Coeur (at Cassou, 11km by D269, and left turn soon after Bon-Encontre) (53.96.10.73). Simple, happy, hospitable restaurant in open country. Flavoursome dishes by Raymond Casse. Meals B–D.
La Corne d'Or (Colayrac, 1.5km west of Agen) (53.47.02.76). Very good cooking, subtle dishes. Meals B–D (E weekdays). Provence, 22 cours 14 Juillet (53.47.39.11). No restaurant. Simple, well-kept hotel; air conditioned. Rooms D–E.
La Rigalette (at Vallon de Véronne, 2km north of Agen by D302) (53.47.37.44). Nice grounds. Good cooking. Meals B–D. Rooms D.

MOISSAC — 82200 Tarn-et-Garonne Le Pont-Napoleon, 2 allées Montebello (63.04.01.55). Edmond Peyre uses best regional products to make excellent regional dishes. Nice atmosphere. Pleasant rooms overlooking river promenade. Several menus. Meals C–E; rooms D–E.

MONTAUBAN — 82000 Tarn-et-Garonne Hostellerie les Coulandrières (at Montbeton, 4km on D958 towards Castelsarrasin) (63.67.47.47). Pleasant modern, built around garden and pool. 3-hectare park. Meals D–E; rooms C.
Orsay et la Cuisine d'Alain, facing station (63.66.06.66). Charming 'minotel'; pretty soundproofed bedrooms. Excellent cooking by Alain Blanc includes Montauban cassoulet. Meals C–E; rooms D–E.

PUYMIROL — 47270 Lot-et-Garonne Les Loges d'Aubergade, 52 rue Royale (53.95.31.46). Lovely 13th-century house and garden. Michel Trama is one of the great cooks of France whose advice is sought by French Railways for TVG trains, Air France for Concorde and Japanese hotels. He blends classic and modern cuisine superbly. Expensive, of course. Meals D (lunch weekdays), A–B; rooms A.

VILLENEUVE-SUR-LOT — 47300 Lot-et-Garonne Hostellerie du Rooy, chemin de Labourdette (53.70.48.48). Probably the best restaurant in the town. Light dishes of local produce. Lovely surroundings. Meals E (weekdays) C–D.
Parc, 13 bd de la Marine (53.70.01.68). Useful Mapotel. Big glassed-in terrace overlooking garden. Imaginative and good cooking. Meals C–E; rooms D.
Auberge de la Toque Blanche (at Pujols, 4km south-west) (53.49.00.30). Best restaurant in the area. Bernard Lebrun uses best regional produce from neighbouring markets and is not afraid of old-fashioned sauces or old-fashioned dishes. Meals E (weekdays)–A.
Hôtel des Chênes (53.49.04.55). Adjoins Toque Blanche by covered way. Charming. Rooms C–D.

Practical information

Tourist Offices (Offices de Tourisme)

Dordogne — Comité Départemental de Tourisme (CDT), 16 rue du Président-Wilson, 24000 Périgueux (53.53.44.35).
Lot — CDT, 107 quai Cavaignac, BP 7, 46001, Cahors (65.35.07.09).
Tarn-et-Garonne, Office de Tourisme, Hotel des Intendants, pl Foch, 82000 Montauban (63.63.31.40).
Lot-et-Garonne — CDT, 4 rue André Chénier, BP 158, Agen (53.66.14.14).

Agen, 107 bd Carnot, Agen 47000 (53.47.36.09).
Bergerac — 97 rue Neuve-d'Argenson, Bergerac, 24100 Dordogne (53.57.03.11).
Brantôme — Mairie, Brantôme, 24310 Dordogne (53.05.70.21).
Brive-la-Gaillarde — pl 14-Juillet, 19100 Corrèze (55.24.08.80).
Cahors — pl A.-Briand, Cahors, 46000 Lot (65.35.09.56).
Montauban — Ancient Collège, pl. Prax, Montauban, 82000 Tarn-et-Garonne (63.63.60.60).
Périgueux — 26 pl. Francheville, Périgueux, 24000 Dordogne (53.53.10.63).
Rocamadour — Mairie, Rocamadour, 46500 Gramat (65.33.62.59).
Rodez — pl Foch, Rodez, 12000 Aveyron (65.68.02.27).
Sarlat — pl Liberté, Sarlat-La-Canéda, 24200 Dordogne (53.59.27.67).
Souillac — 9 bd Malvy, Souillac, 46200 Lot (65.37.81.56).
Villeneuve-sur-Lot — 1 bd de la République, 47300 Lot-et-Garonne (53.70.31.37).

Châteaux and Museums

Brantôme to Brive (pp. 24–45)

BRANTÔME Abbey Monastic Buildings, Mairie (53.05.70.21). Shut Jan.
Fernand Desmoulin Musée, Abbaye (53.05.80.63). Shut Jan; Tues.

BOURDEILLES Château (53.05.73.36). Shut Jan and Tues exc July, Aug.

BORRÈZE Château Salignac–Eyvignes. Open Easter–15th June, 15th Sept.

BRIVE-LA-GAILLARDE Ernest Rupin Musée, 5 rue Dr. Massent (55.24.21.37). Daily exc Sun, holidays.
Edmond Michelet Musée, rue Champanatier. Daily exc Sun, holidays.

HAUTEFORT Château (53.50.40.04). 31 Mar–mid Dec.

JUMILHAC-LE-GRAND Château. English guides. Mid Mar–1st July (check times); 1st July–mid Sept (daily); mid Sept–mid Nov (Sun pm only).

PÉRIGUEUX Musée du Périgord, 22 Cours Tourny (53.53.16.42), archaeology, prehistory. Daily exc Tue.

PUYGUILHEM Château (53.53.44.35/53.54.82.18). 7th Feb–31st Dec. Shut Mon exc July, Aug.

St. CRÉPIN-DE-RICHEMONT Château de Richemont. Daily exc Fri 15th July–31st Aug.

ST. JEAN-DE-COLE Château Marthonie. Daily 1st Jul–31st Aug.

SORGES Maison de la Truffe (Truffle Museum), Eco-Musée de Sorges, Sl (53.05.90.11). Open all year; shut Mon exc July, Aug.

THONAC Château de Losse. End Mar–end Oct.

Bergerac to Sarlat (pp. 47–93)

BERGERAC Winemakers' Guild, Couvent des Récollets, pl de la Myrpe (53.53.44.35/53.22.06.53). Pm 1st Jul–mid Sept.
Musée du Tabac (National Museum of Tobacco) and local history museum, Maison Peyrarède, rue de l'Ancien-Pont (53.57.60.22). Daily exc holidays; pm only Sat, Sun.

BEYNAC Château (53.29.50.40). Daily 1st Mar–31st Nov. Pm Jan, Feb, Dec.

BIRON Château (53.22.62.01). 7th Feb–31st Dec, daily Jul–Aug; daily exc Tue in other months.

CADOUIN Abbey cloisters. Daily exc 1st Jan–8th Feb, and Tue in winter.

DOMME Porte des Tours, pl d'Armes (52.28.37.09). Open by appointment.

FÉNELON Château, Ste. Mondane (part open and Motor Museum) (53.28.71.55). 1st Mar–31st Oct. Shut Tues exc Jul, Aug.

MARQUAY Château Puymartin (53.59.29.97). Daily 1st Apr–31st Oct.

MILANDES Château les Milandes (53.29.50.73). Mid March–early Nov.

MONBAZILLAC Château (53.58.30.27). Daily exc mid Jan–mid Feb.

SARLAT Pénitents Blancs Musée, rue Jean-Jacques Rousseau. Easter–31st Dec. Shut Mon, Sat am exc July, Aug.

Souillac, Rocamadour to St. Céré (pp. 95–117)

CASTELNAU Château (65.38.52.04) Open all year, exc Tue in winter.

ROCAMADOUR Château (65.33.63.29). Open all year.
Musée d'Art Sacré (religious treasures) (65.33.23.23). Check opening times.
Hôtel de Ville, Grande-Rue (65.33.62.59/65.33.63.05 in high season), Lurçat tapestries. 1st Apr–1st Nov, shut Wed exc mid-summer.
Rocher des Aigles (Eagles Rock) (65.33.65.45), breeding centre for birds of prey, with several flying displays each day. Easter–early Nov.

ST. CÉRÉ Casino Gallery (65.38.19.60), Lurçat tapestries and ceramics. Daily.
Château de Montal (65.38.13.72). Daily 1st Mar–31st Oct.
Jean Lurçat Museum, St. Laurent towers. Check opening times.

Cahors and Eastwards (pp. 118–131)

CAHORS Valentré Bridge, Central Tower (65.25.90.56). 1st Jul–31st Aug.
Cathedrale St. Étienne, Cloisters Chapel (65.35.12.30). Daily, exc Sun and holidays, 1st Jul–31st Aug.

CÈNEVIÈRES Château (65.31.27.33). Easter–All Saints Day.

FIGEAC Musée, Hôtel de la Monnaie, pl Vival (65.34.06.25). Open all year.

LABASTIDE-MURAT Murat Musée (65.31.11.86). Daily 1st Jul–30th Sep.

LARROQUE-TOIRAC Château. Daily early Jul–early Sep.

LOCDIEU Abbey and former abbey church. Daily exc Tue 1st Jul–9th Sep.

Montauban to Agen (pp. 133–141)

AGEN Musée, pl Dr. Pierre Esquirol (56.66.35.27). Daily exc Tue.

MONTAUBAN Musée Ingres, 19 rue de la Mairie (63.63.18.04). Daily exc Tue.
Natural History and Prehistory Museum, pl Bourdelle. Daily exc Mon, Sun am and holidays.
Folk Museum, Escolo Carsinolo, pl Bourdelle. Daily exc Sun, Mon and holidays.

VILLENEUVE-SUR-LOT Gaston Rapin Musée (includes Musée de la Prune (Plum Museum)), bd Voltaire. Daily exc Tue, holidays and 20th Sep–20th Oct.

Caves

Brantôme to Brive (pp. 24–45)

Grottes de Villars, Puyguilhem (53.58.82.36). Daily 15th Jun–15th Sep.
Grotte de Rouffignac (Cro de Granville), 5km from les Eyzies (53.05.41.71). Easter–
Nov; daily 1st Jul–15th Sep, Sun only rest of year.
Grotte de Lascaux, Montignac. Not open now, but daily shows in tourist season at
'Lascaux II' reproduction cave. Shut 1st Jan–early Feb. Mon exc July, Aug.

Bergerac to Sarlat (pp. 47–93)

Caverne de Bara-Bahau, Le Bugue (53.06.27.47). 1st Apr–mid Nov.
Gouffre de Proumeyssac, Le Bugue (53.06.28.82). All year exc Jan.
Les Eyzies (several caves with different opening arrangements, see box on p. 22).
Contact SI, pl Mairie (53.06.97.05) for information/opening times.

Souillac, Rocamadour to St. Céré (pp. 95–117)

Grottes de Presque, St. Céré (65.37.87.03). Mid Mar–mid Oct.
Gouffre de Padirac, Padirac (65.33.64.56). 1st Apr–mid Oct.

Cahors and Eastwards (pp. 118–131)

Grotte du Pech-Merle and Amédée-Lemozi Musée (65.31.23.33). Daily Easter–1st
Nov.

Montauban to Agen (pp. 133–141)

Grottes de Lestournelles. 1st Mar–1st Dec. Daily 1st Jun–30th Sep; Sun only rest of
year.
Grottes de Fontirou (53.70.32.35). Daily Easter–Oct; Sun by appointment rest of
year.

Food Markets

Dordogne

Belvès — Saturday; Bergerac — Wed, Sat; Le Bugue — Tue, Sat am; Les Eyzies-de-Tayac (Sireuil) — Mon; Lalinde — Thu; Périgueux — Wed; Rouffignac — Sun; Sarlat — Sat; Terrasson-la-Villedieu — daily; Thenon — Tue; Thiviers — Sat; Vergt — Fri; Villefranche-du-Périgord — Sat.

Lot-et-Garonne

Agen — Wed, Sat, and Sun am; Penne d'Agenais — Sun am; Villeneuve-sur-Lot — Tue, Sat.

Lot

Bretenoux — Tues, Sat; Cahors — Wed, Sat; Castelnau Montratier — Sun; Figeac — Sat; Gourdon — Tues, Sat; Martel — Wed, Sat; Puy L'Eveque — Tues; Souillac — Mon, Wed, Fri; St. Céré — Sat.

Conversion Tables

km	miles	km	miles	km	miles
1	0.62	8	4.97	40	24.86
2	1.24	9	5.59	50	31.07
3	1.86	10	6.21	60	37.28
4	2.48	15	9.32	70	43.50
5	3.11	20	12.43	80	49.71
6	3.73	25	15.53	90	55.93
7	4.35	30	18.64	100	62.14

m	ft	m	ft	m	ft
100	328	600	1,968	1,500	4,921
200	656	700	2,296	2,000	6,562
300	984	800	2,625	2,500	8,202
400	1,313	900	2,953	3,000	9,842
500	1,640	1,000	3,281	3,500	11,483

ha	acres	ha	acres	ha	acres
1	2.5	10	25	100	247
2	5	25	62	150	370
5	12	50	124	200	494

kg	lbs	kg	lbs
1	2.2	6	13.2
2	4.4	7	15.4
3	6.6	8	17.6
4	8.8	9	19.8
5	11.0	10	22.0

°C	°F	°C	°F	°C	°F
0	32	12	54	24	75
2	36	14	57	26	79
4	39	16	61	28	82
6	43	18	64	30	86
8	46	20	68	32	90
10	50	22	72	34	93

Recipes

Farce aux Marrons (chestnut stuffing)

INGREDIENTS (serves 4)

150g raisins	3 tablespoons butter
½kg tinned whole chestnuts	thyme
(or 1kg if using for garnish)	salt, pepper
liver of bird or a few chicken livers	

METHOD

A simple chestnut stuffing for turkey or any poultry or game.

Soak raisins for up to 12 hours; drain chestnuts; chop liver. Cook liver in heated butter for 2 minutes. Remove from pan; add 2 tablespoons butter to pan, add chestnuts, thyme, salt and pepper; cook over medium heat for 5 minutes stirring. Leave to cool. Mix chestnuts, drained raisins and liver together and put inside bird. Roast bird. As garnish, cook another ½kg of chestnuts in butter with salt, pepper and a teaspoon of thyme.

Sauce Périgueux (truffled Périgueux sauce)

Excellent with steak, roast beef, game, poultry, especially guinea fowl, and eaten by gourmets with omelette périgourdine (see below).

INGREDIENTS (serves 4)

30g goose (or duck) fat	30–60g truffles (canned, for juice)
3 chopped shallots	⅓ litre dry white wine
1 sliced onion	1 litre of strong, stock,
15g flour	salt, pepper

METHOD

Cook shallots and onion in the fat until soft, not brown, stir in flour and cook gently, stirring, until slightly brown. Stir in wine, stock, salt and pepper. Bring to boil, simmer uncovered until reduced by half (about an hour). Add juice from truffle can, slice truffles thinly, add them and simmer for 3–4 minutes.

Mousse de Roquefort aux Noix (Roquefort mousse with walnuts)

Though from Rouergue, south of Lot, it is eaten also in Lot often using bleu de Quercy blue cheese.

INGREDIENTS (serves 4)

100g Roquefort cheese	*100g fresh cream*
100g butter	*50g shelled walnuts*

METHOD

Whip the cream. Liquidise cheese and butter, fold carefully into whipped cream. Fold in walnuts and serve.

148

Omelette Périgourdine (omelette with truffles)

INGREDIENTS (serves 4)

8 eggs	1 tablespoon goose fat (or pork)
truffle about egg-size or 2 smaller, chopped in cubes	salt, pepper

METHOD

Housewives put eggs in their shells with truffles in a bag for several hours to impart flavour to eggs. A traditional recipe included small cubes of goose liver as well as truffles.

Beat eggs with salt and pepper. Add chopped truffles (and goose liver if used) and make either one large or two smaller omelettes. If truffles are canned, pour the juice over before serving.

Truffle en Chausson (truffle 'turnover')

INGREDIENTS (serves 4)

Medium to large truffle	For pastry:
100g foie gras (preferably goose; if not, duck)	250g flour
	150g butter
2 thin slices smoked streaky bacon	salt
	beaten egg for glazing

METHOD

Make shortcrust pastry, put in refrigerator for 2 hours, roll out into an even circle. Chop the foie gras. Lay bacon in middle of pastry, spread with chopped liver, put truffle on top, wrap bacon round it; brush edges of pastry with water, fold it over like a turnover. Double fold edges and crimp them with large fork. Brush with beaten egg, place on buttered baking pan. Bake 20 minutes (at 220°C, 425°F, Mark 7). Cover top lightly with foil if in danger of burning.

Mique Sarladaise (dumplings for boiling bacon, salt pork or chicken)

INGREDIENTS (serves 6)

1kg salt pork or bacon	300g stale bread cubes
1 large boiling sausage	salt, pepper
a cabbage, carrots, celery, leek, turnips	3 eggs
	1 tablespoon pork fat

METHOD

Simmer pork in water for 2 hours, add sausage and vegetables. Meanwhile make dumplings by working bread, eggs, pork fat with salt into a dough, rolling into a ball and dusting with flour. Lower into pot with meat and vegetables, cook for 15 mins on each side.

Poule au Pot (country chicken stew)

INGREDIENTS (Serves 4–6 according to size of chicken)

Chicken	500g each of carrots, leeks,
2 tablespoons goose fat	turnips and Swiss chard (*blette* —
(or pork dripping)	leaves of white beet)
1 large onion, chopped	bouquet garni
100g breadcrumbs	1 onion, preferably stuck with
1 clove garlic	3 or 4 cloves
4 egg yolks	

METHOD

This is the recipe which made Henry IV say that every French family should have one each week — takes 3 hours simmering. Use a large boiling fowl (not a young chicken or frozen chicken) with giblets and chicken's blood (if the boucherie will give it to you). Use milk if you cannot get blood.

Soak bread in chicken's blood, add finely chopped liver, heart and gizzard, chopped onion and garlic. Bind with egg yolks, season and stuff chicken with this mixture. Brown chicken on all sides in fat. Cover with boiling salted water and leave to simmer gently (3 hours for big boiling fowl). Vegetables, cleaned and trimmed, should be added for last hour. Serve hot.

Locally, the chicken is often served with a thick green sauce (*sauce verte*) which can be made two ways: by adding mayonnaise to a purée of green herbs (spinach, watercress, parsley, chervil, chives, perhaps tarragon), or by mixing oil and vinegar with finely chopped shallots, chives, parsley, and yolk of hard boiled egg.

Enchaud Périgourdin (roast pork loin with garlic)

Prepare day before

INGREDIENTS *(serves 4)*

1kg boned pork loin,	*200ml water*
keeping the bones	*200ml stock (chicken preferred)*
2 cloves garlic	*sprig of thyme*
30g lard	*salt, pepper*

METHOD

One day ahead, sprinkle pork with salt and pepper, make incisions in the meat and insert thin slivers of garlic. Roll and tie in cylinder. Put in refrigerator overnight.

Next day melt lard in heavy casserole, add pork and bones and roast gently for 30 min (175°C, 350°F, Mark 4), browning meat on all sides. Add water, salt, pepper, thyme, cover and cook for another 1½ hrs until tender. Take out meat and bones. Transfer casserole liquid to a pan and skim off excess fat. Add stock, boil to reduce until strong flavoured. Slice meat, pour sauce over it.

Tourte Quercynoise (Quercy duck-liver tart)

INGREDIENTS (serves 4)

400g duck liver	3 egg yolks
50g truffles	⅛l crème fraiche (cream bought
50g *morels* (dried will do)	slightly soured) or thick cream
75ml Madeira wine	125g flaky pastry made with butter
butter for cooking	salt, pepper

METHOD

Chicken livers could be used but not so authentic.
Slice livers 1cm thick. Slice truffles very thinly. Season. Soak *morels* to wash, then dry. Now soak for several hours in Madeira and truffle juice.
Roll out pastry. Line pie dish, reserve enough for lid of tart. Sweat *morels* in butter, let them cool, place on pastry lining to make a layer, add layer of liver, then layer of truffles. Mix egg yolks and cream with salt and pepper, if canned, add the truffle juice, pour into tart. Put on pastry lid. Cook in oven for 45–50 min (220°C, 425°F, Mark 7). Serve hot.

Les Merveilles (pastry fritters)

INGREDIENTS (serves 4)

500g flour	oil for deep frying
5 eggs	flavouring of your choice
100g butter, softened	(juice of lemon or grated
1 tablespoon baking powder	rind or tablespoon orange
(not essential but makes dish lighter)	flower water or
200g icing sugar	tablespoon brandy)

METHOD

Mix flour, baking powder and eggs in bowl with softened butter, salt and flavouring. Work to a smooth dough, roll out to 6mm thick, cut into strips 15cm long by 2cm wide. Fry pastry strips in deep oil. They puff up and brown quickly. Turn once, take out with a slotted spoon, drain, sprinkle with plenty of icing sugar. Serve hot or keep in airtight tin for snacks.

Index